CRITICAL INQUIRY

CRITICAL INQUIRY

THE PROCESS OF ARGUMENT

MICHAEL BOYLAN

MARYMOUNT UNIVERSITY

A MEMBER OF THE PERSEUS BOOKS GROUP

Published by Westview Press,
A Member of the Perseus Books Group

Find us on the World Wide Web at www.westviewpress.com.

Westview Press books are available at special discounts for bulk purchases in the United States by corporations, institutions, and other organizations. For more information, please contact the Special Markets Department at the Perseus Books Group, 2300 Chestnut Street, Suite 200, Philadelphia, PA 19103, or call (800) 810-4145, ext. 5000, or e-mail special.markets@perseusbooks.com.

Designed by Trish Wilkinson
Set in 11.5-point Janson

Library of Congress Cataloging-in-Publication Data

Boylan, Michael, 1952–
    Critical inquiry : the process of argument / Michael Boylan.
        p.   cm.
    Rev. ed. of: The process of argument. 1988.
    Includes bibliographical references and index.
    ISBN 978-0-8133-4452-2 (pbk. : alk. paper) 1. English language—Rhetoric. 2. Persuasion (Rhetoric) 3. Critical thinking. 4. Language and logic. 5. Reasoning. I. Boylan, Michael, 1952– Process of argument. II. Title.
    PE1431.B67 2010
    808'.042—dc22   2009015178

10 9 8 7 6 5 4 3 2 1

This book is dedicated to my children:
Arianne, Seán, and Éamon.

CONTENTS

PART THREE
RESPONDING TO THE TEXT

PREFACE

This book is in one way the second edition of *The Process of Argument* (Prentice Hall, 1988). However, it is more than just a second edition, but an entirely revised project that is supported by a new publisher, Westview. The first book was designed to be an informal logic text with the intent that it would be used in classes centered around critical thinking—then a nascent field. In fact, the American Association for Higher Education had a session on critical thinking shortly after publication and featured *The Process of Argument* among a few others as examples of how this new field might develop.

After twenty years of continual classroom adoptions, it seems to me that there is good reason to update and reorient the book. The new emphasis is upon how to read and respond critically to argumentative texts. In this way the text has transformed into one that emphasizes critical inquiry through the three r's of *reading*, *reconstructing*, and *responding* to argumentative texts. This is an important skill that is necessary in many courses in the curriculum. For example, in philosophy all the texts presented are argumentative so that this book can instruct the student in achieving the requisite skills needed to read and analyze texts. But these skills are not confined to philosophy. In literature classes, it is commonplace to teach two sorts of essays: (a) the expository (or research) essay and (b) the argumentative essay. This book would be useful for courses in the latter domain. It might also be useful for upper-level literature courses that want to incorporate *critical theory*. This is because the bounds of critical theory are the logically acceptable categories of deductive and inductive reasoning (both represented here). Students of composition classes as well as upper-level theory classes could profit from exposure to a succinct handbook on argument—including rules on understanding, reconstructing, and responding to the same.

Other classes in the curriculum such as politics, economics, and business also require facility in confronting argument successfully. The crossover between disciplines respecting argument is very high. For fourteen years I have led a faculty seminar on ethics and logical argument to professors across the disciplines. This book reflects my experiences. I have also used this method of teaching argument when I was first an English literature teacher in 1976 and later, a philosophy teacher from 1979 onward. So this book also represents thirty-two years of classroom experience.

The presentation is divided into three parts: reading the text, reconstructing the text, and responding to the text (the three r's). In reading the text students are presented with critical tools so that they might not simply accept the text as given. Instead, students are encouraged to go through some self-examination that will enable them to understand their own critical standpoint. This is essential in order that they might be able to ascertain what the speaker is saying and subsequently whether the presentation is correct. I should point out that in the first two sections of the book there is a presentation of how to confront media claims as well as those from the traditional written word.

In reconstructing the text the student is presented with a self-contained system of informal logic. The rules are few and focused on the practical outcomes of enabling the student to confront an argumentative text and to reconstruct the important arguments contained within. These reconstructed arguments are formally presented according to the rules of the system. By making students go through this process, they are forced to give an interpretation of the logical argument contained within. This constitutes another level of understanding that will facilitate better critical inquiry.

Finally, there is the level of responding to the text. In this case the student is enjoined to write a clear pro or con essay. The point of making this clear decision is to promote straightforward argumentative thinking. This is always best achieved when students must make difficult choices. Many students want to be fence-sitters and avoid taking a stance. But this mars their ability to create clear arguments.

This text thus sees itself as promoting the three r's: reading, reconstructing, and responding to the text. If this book can better facilitate student outcomes in creating argumentative essays, then it will be a success. I welcome teacher feedback for the next edition of this book, which can be sent to Boylan.Critical.Inquiry@gmail.com. Key features of this book include:

- Guidance on how to read a text through self-analysis and social criticism
- Tools on how to reconstruct logical argument in a structured manner
- A step-by-step procedure to move from reading to a reflective packet that allows the student to be in the position to write an argumentative essay
- Guidelines on how to structure an argumentative, pro or con essay

It is the intention of this book to assist the student in this process from the point of opening the book to the time when he or she turns in their essay.

Acknowledgments

In addition to those noted in the first edition, I would like to thank Karl Yambert, my editor, who has helped me realize my vision for the project, and all the rest of the Westview team. My thanks also to the professors who took my faculty ethics seminars where I employed many of the techniques found in this book. Their feedback helped me clarify my thoughts and see what might work in a variety of disciplines. In addition, I need to acknowledge Barry Erdeljon, who gave me some good advice on advertising for Chapters 3 and 6. Finally, I would like to thank those who have been my students over the past thirty-two years. There is no better way to find out what works and what doesn't than through direct interaction with students.

Introduction

Critical inquiry begins by recognizing argument. Argument—what is it? Does it mean someone is angry with someone else? Is it something to avoid? Many people are unacquainted with argument as the logical means of persuasion.

It is obvious to everyone that the power of persuasion is valuable. In ancient Greece people spent large sums of money to possess this rare commodity; with the power of persuasion, they felt they could become successful. Other, less mercenary philosophers, such as Plato and Aristotle, extended the study of argument, developing it from an art into a science.

Indeed, today similar attitudes toward persuasion exist. Executive seminars offer training in the art of leadership, sales, and positive thinking. These really amount to methods of getting your ideas across to someone else. The motivation for these seminars is success and financial gain.

Likewise, in our universities, the disinterested study of persuasion proceeds under the titles of philosophy, rhetoric, and composition. Both their practical and intellectual exercises have one point in common: They both aspire to construct rules whereby one can properly persuade others.

A full-scale treatment of this topic is beyond the scope of this volume. Instead, this text will act as an initiation that will supplement and enrich various courses of instruction. Be that as it may, a few things should be noted about the methodology adopted for this present volume and how it intends to aid the student in acquiring the skill of analytic reading and reasoned evaluation.

The first point is that the purpose of argument, *persuasion*, is not a commodity that exists in isolation. One seeks to persuade within a context. This context can be described by the following elements:

Speaker
Audience
Point of Contention
Argument
Common Body of Knowledge

An example of all these elements working together follows:

Sam wants to persuade Kathy to go to the movies. Kathy smiles but doesn't reply. So Sam lists the great reviews and modestly hints at the advantages of going with him. After all, they're both in the same English class, love literature, and could have so much to talk about!

In this example the speaker is Sam, the audience is Kathy, and the point of contention is "Kathy going to the movie with Sam." The argument addresses both the movie's quality and the scenario of a good time; the common body of knowledge is their shared aesthetic value system.

The reader is encouraged to identify these same elements within the context of arguments he or she may encounter. Familiarity with their separate roles is useful for acquiring competence in the process of argument.

Several points about argument can be made using the simple structure outlined above. Perhaps the most difficult of these five elements to understand is the common body of knowledge. This is because this element consists of a collection of facts and shared assumptions about what counts as a proper way to relate facts to each other and to commonly held social norms. These assumptions form a set of logical rules or procedures, and without them, no conclusions can be drawn from the facts. To show some of the difficulties that can occur in even the simplest cases, let us examine the following three examples of common facts:

1. John is six feet tall.
2. It is uncomfortably hot outside today.
3. General Electric is ripe for a corporate takeover.
4. Big oil companies are evil because they gouge the public for excess profits.

The above examples differ in several respects. In the first one, presumably, we have an objective fact. But what makes it objective? It is because (1) we have an agreed-upon unit of measurement, and (2) John is set against this standard. The first statement refers to an agreed-upon standard by which measurements can be made. This is generally unproblematic, but disagreements are possible even at this level. For example, someone who opted for the metric system might disagree that measurements should be taken in the English system of weights and measures. (Some awkward cases have arisen over just this issue between the United States and the International Track and Field Federation concerning standards of measurement and world records in the high jump and pole vault.) Conversion tables are available, of course, but the point is that even with very straightforward cases, one must make certain assumptions that, themselves, are not subject to dispute. Without these assumptions, no resolution is possible.

The second statement refers to the use of the measurement standard. Suppose we agree to the English system of weights and measures. Then (2) is about the actual measuring of John against a calibrated yardstick. Again, this seems uncomplicated, but problems can arise. It is possible to set up an agreed-upon standard and yet disagree about whether the object in question is most appropriately subsumed under it. Such disputes are not uncommon. For example, legal authorities often are at a loss to decide under which statute to try a criminal. Although the law is clear, its application is not.

Thus, even in such straightforward examples as the first common fact above, there are some possible grounds for disagreement. In order to analyze the dispute, we need to make exact distinctions that can point to where the disagreement lies. Once this is known, a reasoned response and dialogue are possible.

In the second common fact, there is an added factor to be considered: the value judgment of what constitutes "uncomfortably hot." One might agree to a temperature scale and how to read it and still disagree about when to judge a day to be uncomfortably hot. To some this may be seventy-five degrees, while to others it may be ninety degrees. In other words, various theories of what constitutes temperature and how to measure it might be agreed upon, but a value judgment about these facts may also be required. In this case agreement must be reached before the argument may continue.

The first two examples refer to *theory*. Theories contain standards and often sanction judgments connected to these standards.

The third example adds one more level to our model. We may agree about *what* constitutes a corporate takeover, *how* to measure the circumstances (as in the first example), and *when*, in theory, this is a good course of action (the judgment entailed in the second example), but still disagree on whether or not General Electric is in such a position at present. Thus, the judgment necessary to put a theory into practice constitutes the third stage of accepted common facts. This stage deals in particulars because it is directed toward judgments to act. These judgments cannot be considered apart from real circumstances, because the circumstances, together with the relevant theory, are necessary to determine what is to be done.

The fourth example confronts the normative element in the common body of knowledge. A theory of distributive justice is introduced (implicitly). It suggests some range of what is an appropriate and an inappropriate level of corporate profit within the social realm—especially in the case of the economically crucial commodity of oil. One might imagine various communities reacting differently to this example. A laissez-faire capitalist group might believe that there is no such thing as too much profit so long as no laws were broken. A socially concerned capitalist, on the other hand, might demur by saying that the community interests are not advanced by allowing too much profit to go to one company when there are others in the society who are in want.

This fourth example is the most robust of all in demonstrating how all the various layers of the shared community worldview might work together.[1]

All four stages work together sequentially to describe the environmental context of the argument. It is hoped that these brief illustrations will inspire the reader's appreciation of the importance of these stages in the process of argument.

A second important area of inquiry concerns the internal structure of the argument itself. One aspect of this structure is the interdependence between the point of contention and the premises. The argument's entire existence—indeed, its reason for being—is solely to put forth the point of contention (called the *conclusion* when it stands in a finished argument). Because of this singular mission, the argument's character must mirror closely that of the point of contention. This creates a mutual dependence between the two so that knowledge of the argument will allow us to know the point of contention, and knowledge of the point of contention will aid us in discovering the argument.

It is true that for any point of contention several arguments may be constructed that will demonstrate that point, but this does not alter the fact that, as stated, the relationship between the two is very close. One way to explain this is that the argument's *premises* and the point of contention mutually imply each other as cause and effect. Such causes have to do with the form or structure of the argument (what the philosopher Aristotle called the "formal cause").

For example, if one wished to make a claim about the all-time best hitter in baseball, one might put forward the following point of contention: "Ted Williams and Rogers Hornsby were the all-time best hitters in American baseball." The premises to prove this point cannot have an arbitrary character. They must establish criteria upon which one can judge a hitter to be the best hitter. In this way the *genesis* of the premises is an effect arising from the point of contention.

We began with "Ted Williams and Rogers Hornsby were the all-time best hitters in American baseball." In order to be accepted, this point of contention needs sentences that logically support it. These sentences are called *premises*. These premises come to be in order to prove some point of contention (also called a conclusion). Whatever comes to be for the sake of something else, in one sense, can be said to be caused by its originator. The order of genesis refers to the mode through which something comes to be.

In this order the point of contention (conclusion) causes the premises.

To set out a simplified example of such an argument we need to establish a standard first. Obviously, as we have seen, setting such standards is controversial. Let us say that the Triple Crown leader is the most adequate test of an all-around hitter. The Triple Crown measures the three primary categories of hitting: batting average, runs batted in, and home runs. Only two players have ever won the Triple Crown in their leagues more than once: Ted Williams and Rogers Hornsby.

The argument could be set down as displayed in Figure 0.1. Premises 1 through 3 come about from our search to prove point 4 (conclusion). However, seen from the perspective of the finished argument, point 4 is *itself* the effect of premises 1 through 3.[2] That is, if we assent to premises 1 through 3, we must agree with point 4. The conclusion is the effect of premises 1 through 3 being true.

Thus, in the *order of logical presentation* the conclusion is the effect and the premises are the cause. This arrangement is just the opposite of the *order of genesis*. This relationship is set out in Figure 0.2. The consequence of this is that the premises and the point of contention (conclusion) are seen to be interdependent so that each affects the character of the other. Thus, the argument in Figure 0.1, "Ted Williams and Rogers Hornsby are the all-time best hitters in American baseball," and the three premises that precede it can influence each other as cause and effect in the manner suggested in Figure 0.2. The direction of this influence de-

FIGURE 0.1: Sample Baseball Argument

Argument	premise	1. The Triple Crown title is the best measure of all-around hitting in American baseball.
	premise	2. Whoever, over a career, wins the Triple Crown the most times is the best all-time hitter in American baseball.
	premise	3. Ted Williams and Rogers Hornsby are the only players to win the Triple Crown more than once in their careers.
	conclusion	4. Ted Williams and Rogers Hornsby are the best all-time hitters in American baseball.

pends upon what perspective we take: from the order of genesis or from the order of logical presentation.

When we *construct* our own arguments, we are most concerned with the order of genesis. We begin with a statement we're trying to prove and then create premises that will prove it. However, when we are *reading* or *listening* to another's argument, then the order of logical presentation is primary. Keeping these purposes and relationships in mind may help later when we try to engage in each process.

The third point is a caution: Sometimes people try to persuade without employing logical argument. For these individuals, logical argument is supplanted by logical fallacy. The difference between logical argument and logical fallacy is the use of illicit means of persuasion. Now why would one wish to do this? In the first place, it is often more successful in persuading large numbers of people in a shorter time than logical argument. Thus, if one is selling either advertising time on television or space within a magazine, he may receive a quicker return on each dollar by employing logical fallacy rather than logical argument. This need not be the case; advertising *can* pictorially embody logical argument (see exercises in Chapters 3 and 6).

The trouble with fallacies is that they depend upon tricks and illusions. They persuade illegitimately. This does not mean that everyone who employs a fallacy could not have constructed a persuasive message using logical argument. In most cases, the use of fallacy merely indicates the rhetorician's preference.

Thus, Acme Widgets may try to persuade the public to purchase their product by placing it between a pair of attractive male and female models attired in evening clothes. The force of the persuasion is the fact that everyone wants to be young, rich, and attractive. The Acme Widget is *associated* with this pleasing picture by the advertiser, who wants

FIGURE 0.2: The Relationship Between the Elements of Logical Persuasion

ORDER OF GENESIS	ELEMENTS	ORDER OF LOGICAL PRESENTATION
Effect	Premises	Cause
↑		↓
Cause	Conclusion	Effect

us to think that we can become young, rich, and attractive by purchasing the Acme Widget.

However, anyone who was pointedly questioned about this connection would surely demur, because no natural, scientific connection can be found between the two. Everyone would agree to this. But still the ads are successful. Why? Because people often *do not* consciously question what they are seeing. If they did, they would feel insulted that the Acme Company thinks it can sell its widgets without telling us relevant information, such as how its product's features compare with those of its competitors.

It is this unthinking, subliminal reaction that proponents of logical fallacy depend upon. When we fall into their trap, we become slaves to their tricks. Fortunately, there is a way out. The tool is logic. The power is the mind. One of the beneficial by-products of learning the skills set forth in this book is that you will be less likely to be hoodwinked by such illogical shenanigans. By applying reason properly we acquire a power of self-determination. This free autonomy is inherently desirable—and yet it does not come without some training of our natural mental faculties. This will be discussed further in Chapter 2.

The fourth point concerns a further incentive for understanding the structure of argument. We all wish, at times, to offer opinions on various questions. Someone sets down an argument such as the one I did on baseball batters. Perhaps you disagree with the argument. What response are you to make? One thing you might say is, "That's all wrong!" or "You're crazy!" But such responses don't convey any specific content other than the fact that, upon hearing the argument, you were put into a negative state of mind.

But unless we can get beyond that point, no discourse is possible. Also, it may be that there is no real disagreement at all, but merely a problem in the way the sentence was expressed.

The tool that allows one to make real progress is *logical analysis*. Analysis literally means "to break up." Therefore, when presented with a composite whole, one must isolate the various parts: speaker, audience, point of contention, argument, and common body of knowledge.

Once analysis has revealed the structure and relationship of these parts, one can look at each part separately and make individual evaluations. It is possible, for example, that one may agree with every premise except one. In this case, all discussion should be focused upon that single point. For if this point can be resolved, then accord is possible. Using our baseball example, such a process might look like the following:

A Dialogue Between Sue and Tom

TOM: Ted Williams and Rogers Hornsby are the greatest hitters of all time.

SUE: No way.

TOM: It's true.

SUE: How do you figure that?

Tom then provides the argument from Figure 0.1.

SUE: Now I see why you think Ted Williams and Rogers Hornsby are so great. But I disagree with your point that whoever wins the Triple Crown the most times in his career is the all-time best hitter.

TOM: You got a better idea?

SUE: Sure. Home runs. It's obvious. Every fan knows the hardest thing to do is to send the ball over the fence.

TOM: Well, I don't know. If that's true, then Barry Bonds and Henry Aaron would be the greatest hitters of all time.

SUE: Exactly!

In this dialogue the single point upon which they disagree becomes the topic of discussion. Space does not allow a full investigation of the merits of the point at issue, but it is important that Tom and Sue realize where their disagreement lies: the definition of the all-time best hitter. (The disagreement concerns which measurement standard to use—see our discussion under the first point.)

Finding the crucial point is what analysis is all about. It allows one to see the structure of the argument. Just as scientists search for the critical experiment to prove or disprove their theories, so also the logically minded person searches for critical premises in the argument. Chapters 1–3 will present ways to read critically in order to discover which premises are critical to the argument. Chapters 4–6 will set out the rules for such analysis, while Chapters 7–9 will discuss the ways to formulate reactions to the arguments once they are set out.

The general principle we're operating under is this: One cannot offer a meaningful and valid opinion on a point of contention unless he or she has first engaged in logical analysis. Otherwise, the reaction will be hopelessly vague and of no value.

For example, if someone asks you how you liked a movie and you reply, "It was good" or "It stunk," you are giving very little meaningful information. Perhaps your measurement standard for judging movies depends upon how many characters are killed in the plot: More than ten killings rates a positive response; less than ten a negative one. Obviously, then, without knowing the measurement scale and the value judgments made from that scale, any response given is almost meaningless.

In these brief remarks I have touched upon some of the basic features of logical argument and why it is of such importance to become competent at it. Throughout our lives we are constantly bombarded with points of contention—whether it is an agreement to buy a car, negotiating a raise, responding to a business memo, writing a letter to the editor, or just being an articulate, autonomous human being. There is power in understanding the rules and structure of argument. This potent capacity has been recognized since the time of the Ancient Greeks. They sacrificed greatly to gain these mysterious gifts because they believed them to be of enduring and inherent value.

These pages seek to initiate the reader into an acquaintance with this power.

Reading Questions

1. What are the elements that make up the context of argument?
2. Give an example of all these elements working together.
3. Name the four ways by which facts may be disputed via the common body of knowledge.
4. How do the orders of *genesis* and *logical presentation* differ?
5. Why do people employ logical fallacies?
6. How should one confront logical fallacy?

Notes

1. I set out the structure and consequences of the common body of knowledge in more detail in *A Just Society* (Lanham, MD, and Oxford: Rowman and Littlefield, 2004), Chapter 5.

2. Premises and conclusions are really abstract ideas whose truth is independent of what we believe or assent to. However, beliefs and motives are crucial to the way we construct arguments (*order of genesis*), and they provide useful tools for describing the *order of logical presentation*.

PART ONE

READING
THE TEXT

CHAPTER 1

Confronting the Text

The first step is actually to open the book. For some this is a tough measure, but you cannot begin to confront a text that *you* do not *engage*. From that moment onward, you must pay heed. Reading is not all that easy. This chapter will be a primer on how to confront and engage the text. I will give acknowledgment of various learning styles and how they might best be accommodated.

The second step is to read your given selection from beginning to end without stopping (presuming that the argumentative selection assigned is thirty pages or less). The reason shorter passages work better is that reading argumentative texts is very difficult and involves multiple readings. When assigning an entire book to read, I try to break it up into chapters that are more manageable. If a student has a thirty-page assignment for class and has to read it four or five times, then it's really a 120- to 150-page assignment. Since argumentative texts require a high comprehension level, reading them in smaller doses at a time is more manageable.

The third step is to ascertain what the general point is and where the text might be parsed into sections for analysis. If you read with a pencil, you can make the markings in your text. If you are an auditory learner, then you might consider dictating to yourself the principal divisions in the text. At the end of the third step, you should have some general ideas about what the text is arguing and how it is structured. This generally takes at least two readings.

The fourth and final step in the reading phase is to uncover the point of contention (conclusion) and the premises that support it (including adding suppressed premises necessary to make the argument complete). More discussion of the formal reconstruction of the argument will be presented in the next part of the book. Here we are concerned with detecting where the conclusion and supporting argument are. Beginners in confronting the text often have problems identifying the conclusion and its supporting material. Here are some suggestions based upon learning style:

A. For traditional learning styles, try underlining or highlighting or annotating the text so that you might better interact with it to ascertain its principal meaning and how the point of contention is supported.

B. For students who are more social learners, you might consider forming a study group to go over this fourth step in a social setting (with peer interaction).

What follows are practical suggestions for overcoming these difficulties based upon confronting the text.

Identifying Conclusions and Premises

The most common problem in reconstructing arguments in the form of a logical outline is determining just what a premise is and what a conclusion is. Often the text appears opaque, and you have to struggle to find its structure. As mentioned earlier, you must first discover the conclusion. The best way to do this is by becoming sensitive to the thematic context: Ask yourself key questions after reading a passage, such as: Why did the author write this? What was the author's intention? What was the author trying to prove?

If these questions do not point you to something immediately, then try two other tricks:

A. Pretend you are a reporter writing a story on the author's ideas. What would make a good headline for your feature?

B. Pretend you are an attorney in a trial. The author is the opposing attorney and is making a case before the jury. You must discover the main point of the opposing argument so you can respond.

Those of you in study groups can set yourselves into dramatic situations (such as a courtroom drama within the study group) to try to make this clearer. I have also had students who were very artistically visual and who were able to sketch pictures of the argument's conclusion and the support of the same. One student drew me a picture of a rose garden with the rosebuds being the conclusion, and the stems, leaves, and soil being various aspects of the argument's support. The parts of the sketch were then annotated with sentences or sentence fragments that translated back to the original text.

These questions and imaginary situations are merely devices to help the reader become sensitive to the thematic context. This context, including what comes before and after, can place you in the proper interpretive position to ascertain with confidence the point of contention.

From the thematic context the conclusion should readily become clear. It is the *point of the passage*. Once the point has been determined, you can ask questions such as: How is this point being supported? What is the proof? The answers to these questions should supply the premises of the argument, providing the reasons for accepting the point of the passage.

All of the above suggestions merely represent ways to get at the main point of an argument and its accompanying support. The reader is encouraged to think of other methods that might work. Try these in exercises that follow this section of the chapter.

In short, the following method is preferred:

Thematic Context—Plan A

A. The point of the passage = conclusion
B. Reasons for accepting the point of the passage = premises

Word Clues—Plan B

If you are still baffled by some passage, then you may want to see if any verbal clues exist. Verbal clues are key words that often signify conclusions or premises. These words are signals that can be useful when all else fails. For example, the following words and phrases often indicate a conclusion:

Word Clues for Conclusion

therefore, hence, thus, consequently, so, it follows that, it must be that, we may infer that, necessarily, now we can see that, it is now evident that, shows that, indicates that, proves that, entails that, implies that, establishes that, allows us to believe that

What follows these words is generally a conclusion. If these words occur near the beginning or end of a paragraph, it is likely that you have reached the conclusion of the argument contained within the entire paragraph. (Of course, some arguments continue for several paragraphs or pages.)

Word Clues for Premises

The following words and phrases generally signify the presence of a premise:

because, so, since, in order to, for the reason that, for, assuming that, is shown by, is indicated by, is proven by, is entailed by, is implied by, is established by, in that, due to the fact that, given that, may be concluded from, inasmuch as

What follows these words is generally a premise or a group of premises.

Word Clues for Both

The word *so* can tip off either a conclusion or a premise depending on how it is used, as in the following:

> *"So" as premise indicator:* We'll buy eggs today so we don't have to go the store tomorrow, which is a holiday.
>
> *"So" as a conclusion indicator:* It is raining. We hate getting wet, so let's take an umbrella.

Mixed Mode—Plan C

In many passages the thematic context is not clear. But there are no verbal clues from the list. What do you do then? Resort to Plan C.

One final way to determine the argumentative structure when the first two plans fail is to engage in calculated guessing and then try inserting the words from the two word clue groups at the appropriate spot in the text (before the suspected conclusion or premise). Does the result make sense? If it does, then it is very likely that you have uncovered the argumentative structure of the text. Your hypothesis is either confirmed or disconfirmed.

For example, consider this passage:

Maggie became skinny. She had suffered an emotional loss over the death of her father, and food no longer tasted good to her.

   Guess at the conclusion: Maggie became skinny.

   Confirmation with word clues: "Because" after the conclusion should indicate premises.

   Thus, Maggie became skinny *because* she had suffered an emotional loss over the loss of her father and food no longer tasted good.

The new paragraph makes sense; therefore the hypothesis is confirmed.

   Resulting outline:

1. Maggie suffered an emotional loss over her father's death—(fact)
2. Food no longer tasted good to Maggie—(fact)

---

3. Maggie lost weight—(1, 2)

This last approach is called the mixed mode. It is used when one cannot fully determine premises and conclusions by the thematic context method, and there are no word clues.

   A summary of these three methods follows:

   Plan A: Thematic Context. The point of the passage is the conclusion. The reasons for accepting the point of the passage are called the premises.

Plan B: Word Clues. These are various words and phrases that often signal the presence of premises and conclusions.

Plan C: Mixed Mode. In difficult passages in which the context does not help to positively identify premises and conclusions in which there are no word clues, try substituting some of the word clues in crucial sections of the text. If the sense remains the same, then the inserted words will help you identify premises and conclusions.

The first level of confronting the text is to obtain a general overview of what is in the given selection (first reading). The next level is to search for the general point of the passage and discover the point of contention that is at the heart of argumentative passages (second reading). Once one has discovered the point of contention, it is now requisite to ascertain what body of the text supports the conclusion. These reasons why constitute the premises. Let's stop for a moment and practice these skills.

Exercises

Directions: Identify the conclusion and the premises.

Group A

1. China is the largest country in the world. The United States can use all the allies it can get. Thus, the United States should cultivate China's friendship and support.

2. "The road less taken" has made all the difference because I am not a man whose nature it is to follow the crowd, and the other road represents the direc-

tion that most people choose. It makes all the difference when you are true to your nature.

3. Tom Brady, quarterback for the New England Patriots, will be one of the top quarterbacks in NFL history, assuming that he remains as productive in the future as he has been in the past and that the quarterback rating system is a true indicator of a quarterback's relative talent. Up to now Brady is near the top of the NFL's quarterback rating system.

4. Terrorists, by definition, are murderers since they prey upon innocent civilians who are not directly involved with their dispute. People who kill innocents are murderers. Al Qaeda continues to support terrorists, and those who support some group must take some responsibility for that group's actions. Consequently, al Qaeda's leaders must share in the responsibility for terrorist incidents.

Group B

1. Brad Pitt is a great film star. He has starred with famous talents such as Angelina Jolie and George Clooney. His films have always made money and have drawn critical acclaim. Who would deny the attraction he holds over women of all ages? These are the markings of a true star.

2. High-tech expertise is the highest demonstration of human knowledge. Today, civilization has achieved a level of high-tech expertise that is unmatched in history. Truly, we are the most brilliant group of humans in history. (declaration of a former student)

3. No one wants the world to end. But just as true, no one wants our country to be conquered by military force. Disarmament talks involve a difficult balancing act. The stakes are high, but something must be done to represent both poles of opinion.

4. Most of the interstate highway system has roadways that were designed to handle traffic going 80 mph. We should raise the speed limits on the interstate highway system. What a waste to drive 65 mph on roads designed to be navigated safely at 80 mph! The gas savings at 65 are minimal. Besides, no one obeys this law anyway. And laws that no one obeys breed disrespect for law in general. Nobody wants that—to paraphrase a popular argument.

Using Suppressed Premises

The next step after one has mastered finding the conclusion and the premises is to confront the text in a different and subtler way. This involves questioning the author on the premises provided and whether they are sufficient to generate the conclusion for which he or she is arguing. Often it is the case that the premises that are actually set down on the page are insufficient to generate the conclusion. In these cases the reader is meant to supply the missing premises automatically as he or she is reading. These suppressed premises, or enthymemes, exist because it is often cumbersome to set out each and every premise in a prose argument. Certain points that seem trivial or are easily supplied by the mind are generally omitted.

If, for example, a mayoral candidate said, "Experience counts; vote for John Doe," the suppressed premise would be, John Doe has experience. Without this premise the argument is invalid, but the suppressed premise is easily supplied by the mind.

However, as we will see in Chapter 2, the possibility of logical fallacy requires an active level of vigilance. It is easy to be fooled when the stated argument becomes complicated. Thus, there is a necessity to be exact in the reconstruction of persuasive argument including suppressed premises.

Sometimes people express anxiety over the fact that they feel they are pulling suppressed premises out of "thin air." They feel that such a procedure is too random and undermines the objective character of the argument.

To these people I reply that not *every* additional premise will be allowed, but only those that (a) meet a formally observed inferential gap, (b) are in the spirit of the general argument, and (c) do not contradict any other avowed position of the author. By observing these three cautions, one can avoid misrepresenting the author by substituting one's own argument for the author's.

In trying to meet these three requirements ask yourself: What is necessary to complete this argument? If you can make the substitution observing the above cautions, do so. It is only by representing complete arguments that we can accurately determine whether or not they are correct.

Note: As a matter of form, put suppressed premises into brackets so that others will understand that these are your additions. Our above example would thus be reconstructed as:

1. Experience counts—(assertion)
[2. John Doe has experience—(fact)]

_____

3. Vote for John Doe—(1, 2)

In order to develop your skill at finding and inserting suppressed premises (enthymemes) when they are needed, complete the following exercises. (Please note that sometimes what is suppressed is not a premise, but the conclusion itself.)

Exercises

Directions: Supply the missing sentence whether it is a premise or a conclusion. Put your missing sentence in brackets.

Group A

1. No enthymemes are complete, so this argument is incomplete.
2. Ezra Pound made fascist broadcasts. Therefore, after the war he was imprisoned.
3. I have two tickets for the game tonight. We like each other, and we like basketball.
4. Only members may use this tennis court. You will have to go away.
5. You can't borrow my car. I only lend it to good drivers.
6. Abortion means you have killed a fetus. Abortion is impermissible.

7. Abortion means a woman has made a choice about her body. Abortion is permissible.

Group B

1. "Lovers may never possess all of another's love, for to be a lover is fervently to desire possessing all of another's love. But the heart daily grows in its capacity to love."—Adapted from "Lovers' Infiniteness" by John Donne

2. Fred says that he believes in every word in the Bible exactly as it is written. Further, Fred claims that every Christian must serve God. One thing that is written is that "Man cannot serve both God and Mammon." It follows that Fred is not a Christian.

3. "Orestes: You don't see them, you don't—but I see them: They are hunting me down—hence the soul cannot be possessed of the divine union until it is divested itself of the love of created beings."
   —Adapted from *Sweeney Agonistes* by T. S. Eliot (Hint: Orestes's soul is not divested of the love of created beings.)

Conclusion

The point of this chapter is to help the student formally confront a text with the purpose of finding first the conclusion and then the support of that conclusion—the premises. This process includes adding premises (or the conclusion) in the spirit of the argument as you understand it via several readings of the text. Various suggestions about confronting the text from different learning styles were also put forth. At this point, we have been engaged in a rather formal exercise. The next step is to bring you into the picture. Enter Chapter 2!

Critical Reading

Worldviews, Fallacies, and the Common Body of Knowledge

Once a person has read an argumentative text and decided on the point of contention as well as the support for the same, the next step is to begin the critical process of evaluating the argument. How does one do this authentically? The answer requires a return to the reader's own personal worldview (the sum of his or her normative and factual understandings of the world).

It is this author's contention that one of the most important ways that any of us can assess truth claims is via our worldview perspective, which is formulated in normative terms, but also applies to our epistemological duties.[1] I see two sorts of imperatives by which each of us is constrained as we formulate who we are and how we are to exist in the world. The first of these is the personal worldview imperative: "*All people must develop a single comprehensive and internally coherent worldview that is good and that we strive to act out in our daily lives.*"[2] This imperative has four parts. First, it exhorts completeness. Theories of ethics or theories about truth must be complete. That means that they must deal with all possible cases brought to them in such a way that an answer can be generated mechanically from the system adopted. If a case could be brought forward in which no answer could be formulated (in principle), then it would invalidate the system.

Second, coherency is required. This means that no internal contradictions are allowed.[3] If one were to criticize an author from two inconsistent standpoints, this would violate this dictum. One must take some time to ascertain where her critical position comes from—what it allows and what it forbids. This is important both from an ethical and from an epistemological (theory of knowledge) perspective.

Third, there is the issue of connection to a theory of good. *Theory of good* refers to one of the accepted moral theories: intuitionism, non-cognitivism, contractarianism, virtue ethics, utilitarianism, and deontology.[4] It is important to have some sensibility about what you believe to be good because the good and the true overlap in many respects.

Fourth is the condition that the principle involved applies to the world. In the terms of theories of truth, this is an exhortation of some pragmaticism. This does not commit the student to hold pragmaticism as his or her principal theory, but it does require an affirmation of some connection to the world in which the alleged truths are said to apply.

The personal worldview imperative acts like a tune-up to the engine of our minds to make sure that the engine is running properly—meaning that we have given assent to what we hold to be true and good. These two dispositions are crucial in order to formulate a critical standpoint.

However, there is one more role that we must consider: our role as a member of various communities. The smaller, micro-communities, are the ones we must think about first because they affect us proximately in our daily living. These communities include our family, our friends, our school, our sports team, our church/mosque/synagogue, and so forth. Generally the size of this community is 500 people at maximum. It is the size of a group with whom we can be personally acquainted.

We also belong to various macro-communities, such as our city, state, nation, hemisphere, and the world. The community standpoint also requires some direction. I call this the shared community worldview imperative: *Each agent must contribute to a common body of knowledge that supports the creation of a shared community worldview (that is itself complete, coherent, and good) through which social institutions and their resulting policies might flourish within the constraints of the essential, core, commonly held values (ethics, aesthetics, and religion).* This imperative is analogous to the personal worldview imperative. It exhorts one to affirm openly their community membership and to be an active, tolerant, and facilitating member.[5]

When one reads an argumentative text, it is important that, in addition to one's thoughtful and clear personal worldview, he or she includes membership in various communities so that a more rounded understanding of the individual comes forth. From these two standpoints, the reader is in a better position to formulate a critical perspective that resonates.

For example, take Angela Ayala (an immigrant Latina philosophy student). She may have to sort out issues in her personal worldview between what she held to be true in her birth country and in the United States. There may be some cultural dissonances she needs to work out. Until she does this, her critical perspective will be underdeveloped.

Or take Jamal, an African American student who has lived in an impoverished section of society that looks at the television and the Internet and sees everything that is denied to him. He must come to terms with his community worldview perspective before he can confront his personal worldview (though both interact).

Then there is Mary Smythe. She is a privileged person of European descent who is from a family that has been in the United States since the Revolutionary War. She doesn't see people like Angela or Jamal; they are invisible to her. But they might not be invisible were she to undergo the personal and shared community worldview imperative challenge.

What is necessary is that each agent examines his or her personal and community worldview perspective in order to ascertain whether it is what they really believe (and not some artifact of his or her scattered personal development). The following exercises are designed to go a little way in that direction.

Exercises

Group A: The Personal Worldview

1. What are your most deeply held moral convictions? (List no more than five.)
2. How would you describe the natural world as you understand it? (List no more than seven.)
3. What are the greatest challenges to you personally in living the good life? (List no more than ten.)
4. How do your convictions affect the way that you judge others?

Group B: The Community Worldview

1. List the three most important (micro-) communities in which you feel attachment.
2. How active are you in your communities? How much do your communities allow you to be involved?
3. How would you revise these communities if you had the power?
4. What is your relationship to larger (macro-) communities? (List at least three.)

Logical Fallacies

Once one has considered his or her worldview standpoints, it is important to become aware of the various false claims for recognition. These are generally called logical fallacies. Most books on persuasion contain some catalog of logical fallacies. However, there is no uniform agreement upon which fallacies ought to be introduced or upon how to group them—even the exact definition of a particular fallacy may vary from text to text. There is no unanimity.

That aside, several things can be said about logical fallacies. First, a logical fallacy is an argument. As an argument it can be outlined. Second, logical fallacies *are* powerful persuaders. They shouldn't be, but they are. These arguments should not persuade, because they are bad arguments. But what makes them bad? The reason logical fallacies are bad is that they pretend to be logical. Reliance upon logical persuasion is essential to our human nature. When we consciously choose to use fallacy to persuade others, we degrade ourselves. When we negligently allow ourselves to be duped by logical fallacy, we similarly degrade ourselves. As said earlier, we have a duty to defend ourselves in our autonomous acceptance of our personal and community worldview. Thus it is of critical importance that we acquaint ourselves with the most important logical fallacies.

Logical fallacy is quite prevalent. Many arguments that one encounters are logical fallacies. These are evaluated in the same general manner as described in Part Two.

Much can be and has been written on logical fallacy. My purpose here is to provide a mere glimpse of the operation of this pretender. What will be presented is enough to prepare the student for encountering this all-too-frequent form of persuasion in order that he or she may be able to combat it through an appropriate evaluation.

Like logical argument, logical fallacy seeks to persuade. The problem is that its means are not legitimate. It uses tricks and sleights of hand to distract and confuse while the audience is being manipulated. To be manipulated by another is to become that person's slave. None of us would prefer to be slaves. Thus a few remarks on the types of fallacies and how to uncover them with an outline are instructive. Here is one classification of the logical fallacies.

Shifting the Grounds

This first classification of logical fallacy has to do with rearranging the grounds of the premises. A case is assembled on a premise that is not directly relevant to the conclusion. This kind of fallacy has several variations.

Argument Against the Speaker (Argumentum Ad Hominem)

Let us assume for our sample a situation in which the Allied commanders in World War II were discussing the invasion of Normandy. In the interests of historical accuracy we will not identify the interlocutors, such as General George Marshall or General Alan Brooke. Rather, we will just say General A, General B, and so on.

Example One

GENERAL A: I think an invasion of France near Bayeux might be a good idea. It would afford the least resistance and militarily would be the most defensible.

GENERAL B: You Yankees don't know anything about it. You're from across the Atlantic. Besides, you're always hot for harebrained schemes—it's that gambling blood inherited from all those cowboys of yours.

Comment: General B has not offered a proper, logical evaluation of General A's argument. Instead, General B has tried to shift the grounds of the argument away from General A's plan to the general himself. Unless a person's character or circumstances are functionally relevant to the argument at hand, they should not be raised. This can readily be seen when we try to outline General B's argument.

1. To know geographic facts relevant to a military operation requires one to have lived near the site in question—(assertion)
2. General A has not lived near France—(fact)
3. General A should not opine about a military operation in France—(1, 2)
4. A person's ability to make a rational decision is dependent on the clear thinking of all that nation's people—(assertion)
5. Some American cowboys were not clear thinkers—(fact)
6. No American should be trusted to make a rational decision—(4, 5)

---

7. No American should consult on a European invasion—(3, 6)

When set out in this way, the stupidity of premises 1 and 4 becomes clear. But often this form of fallacy is persuasive. An audience can quickly forget the topic at hand when an attack is begun against the speaker. It is perhaps for this reason that *argumentum ad hominem* is a favorite among politicians.

Argument by Coercion (Argumentum Ad Baculum)

Example Two

GENERAL A: If you don't think our plan is the right way to invade the continent, remember we can take our support elsewhere. And without our support, you'll be invaded in a week.

Comment: This argument contains a fallacy. It becomes apparent after outlining.

1. Above all else, Britain does not want to be conquered by the Nazis—(assertion)
2. At the time of speaking, the only thing stopping the Nazi invasion is the presence of U.S. forces in England—(assertion)
3. U.S. presence is contingent upon Britain accepting the Americans' D-day proposal as the best plan—(assertion)

4. Britain will accept the U.S. D-day proposal as the
   best plan—(1–3)

From the outline it is clear that Britain's acceptance of the
D-day proposal as the best plan comes not from the proposal's military merits, but from the United States' threat. The
grounds of argument have been shifted to a point of power
leverage. This blackmail is common to the various forms of
argumentum ad baculum. It is not a logical form of persuasion. It depends upon the idea that "might makes right."

Similarly, the other fallacies that involve shifting the
grounds of argument may be outlined and found logically
irrelevant to the stated point of contention. The reader is
invited to construct his or her own outline to prove this.
Below are brief descriptions of other logical fallacies that fit
under the general classification of shifting grounds.

Argument from Ignorance

This fallacy rests on the notion that a proposition is true
simply because it has never been proven false, and vice versa.

Example Three

No one conclusively has proven ESP false. Therefore, it
must be true.

Comment: Just because there have been no successful proofs
that ESP is false does not demonstrate that it cannot be

proven false. Maybe we have not been inventive enough in our examinations of ESP. The premise only shows that it is still an open question.

Appeal to Pity

The vehicle of persuasion here is emotion. The functional facts are disregarded in favor of overpowering sentiment. Thus a lawyer or senator may make his case on the basis of some irrelevant plea.

Example Four

You should not convict my client because he has led a difficult life full of disappointment.

Or, We should save the Heritage Clock Company because it has been a part of all our lives since we were children. How can we allow a fixture of our past to go under?

Comment: Neither of these arguments addresses the facts. They depend upon such specious, suppressed premises as whoever has many disappointments may be excused from living according to the law, or all cherished institutional fixtures of our past should be preserved. When outlined with all the requisite premises, these illogical premises become obvious. Those who do not engage in outlining may very well find themselves hoodwinked by this powerful mode of persuasion.

Social Identification

This is one of the forms most frequently used in advertising. It is sometimes called "keeping up with the Joneses." If the persuader can convince you that everyone is doing something, then the reader is drawn to conforming. Perhaps this natural tendency comes from some deep, biological origin rooted in our being social animals. But this, of course, says nothing about what logically ought to be the case.

One can include in this type of fallacy all non-logical identifications based on a me-too principle. An example might be the association of a product with a well-dressed model in front of a Rolls-Royce. Yet no one would agree with the premise that anyone who purchases product x will drive a Rolls and be successful and happy. It is ludicrous when stated as such.

Still, this fallacy is based on some social identification akin to this. The source of this feeling is similar to one everyone knows: When the entire room rises to give a standing ovation, it is difficult to resist joining in—even if you don't agree that the performance deserved it. Social identification is one of the most powerful primitive forces that influence human behavior. Since it is so powerful, it is even more important to try to outline such forms and expose this sort of fallacy when it occurs.

Authority

There are two forms of this fallacy: disconnected and connected.

Disconnected authority refers to authorities in one area being used to support a position or product in an area foreign to their expertise. Thus a baseball player may be used to promote a breakfast cereal, or a rock star may be used to support a political cause. In each case, the force of persuasion is that someone who knows something about one area will know something about all areas. This is obviously false. One's respect for an authority's expertise is not logically transferable.

Connected authority occurs when one accepts a point of contention *merely* because an authority says so. Even if the source is an expert in that field, one should not accept a conclusion *just* because an authority asserts it. For example, Mr. Smith may be an expert in ethics, but one should not accept his judgment that abortion is moral or immoral *just* because he says so. What is required is an argument along with it. It is the *argument* that should persuade, not merely an authority.

Now, it is true that not every point can be traced to its origins. Sometimes we must accept certain points without thorough analysis. In these cases, connected authority is generally more reliable than unconnected authority or no authority, but it should always be accepted that the use of an authority creates a contingent chain that is open to question. The longer the chain, the greater the possibility for error. This caveat should always be kept in mind when using argument from connected authority.

Begging the Question

One effective way to shift the grounds of the argument is to beg the question. Traditionally, this has been defined as assuming what you are trying to prove.

Example Five

Opium produces sleep because of its dormitive powers. (Molière poking fun at Aristotelian science.)

Comment: What is at question is *why* opium causes people to sleep. But the reason given is that opium has sleep-producing powers. This is precisely what is at issue. The premises do not prove the point of contention. Thus begging the question is an illegitimate type of argument. What tips one off to begging the question is the presence of premises that, instead of causing the conclusion, actually depend upon the conclusion for their own veracity. Beware of premises that seem to be merely a restatement of the conclusion.

Changing the Question

In this form you shift the grounds of the argument away from the issue under discussion and to another issue that you can answer. For example, if someone asked a vice-president for marketing why sales were down, the vice-president might reply by detailing the advertising campaign used in the past year. The question was not about the ad campaign, but about the dip in revenue. Thus the grounds for the argument have been shifted.

The shift in attention can occur in the premises or in the conclusion itself. When it occurs in the premises, the speaker redefines the question into an entirely different issue (as in the above case). When the change occurs in the conclusion, the conclusion does not follow from the premises. (This is often called irrelevant conclusion.)

Example Six

STUDENT: You can't flunk me, Ms. Hightower.

MS. HIGHTOWER: Why not? You flunked all your assignments.

STUDENT: You can't flunk me because I need a good grade to stay on the volleyball team. Besides, I really liked your class.

Comment: The premises in this case have nothing to do with the conclusion. The student has changed the question from what he deserves to *what would be convenient.*

Often someone employing this type of argument fallacy rambles on and on, hoping the audience will forget the original point of contention. Then he draws his conclusion. But upon outlining such an argument, it will be found that the inferences are loose, and the premises do not interlock. Outlining will make the shift apparent.

Dilemma Question

This fallacy focuses attention away from the principal issue by offering a false choice. Because the choice appears to be exhaustive, it makes an insinuation that it has no business making. A classic example is the old joke: Have you stopped beating your wife yet? Either answer of yes or no is misleading. The same is true of the slogan, Would you rather fight the war on terrorism here in the United States or in some foreign country? There is no logical reason why these are the real alternatives.

For example, there might be a Senate debate about sending U.S. troops to some foreign country to fight terrorism. An advocate of the deployment might ask an opponent, "Would you rather have terrorist attacks in the United States or are you willing to fight for your freedom?" The implication is that unless troops are deployed, the country in question—and eventually the United States—will be the victim of countless acts of terrorism. This shifts the emphasis away from whether this particular deployment is prudent and will, in fact, do what it is claimed it will do.

The focus of the argument should be on the *means* of attaining the objective that all would agree upon. However, the argument is shifted away from that focus and onto the goals themselves. The means are assumed and linked to general goals to which all agree by creating a false dilemma. The attention of the argument is focused away from where it should be.

Repetition

The truth of a proposition is not affected by the number of times it is asserted—even though repetition may psychologically make it seem plausible to the audience. Each assertion of a proposition is an independent event and should be evaluated as such.

Example Seven

POLITICIAN A: If you elect my opponent, Politician B, you will receive endless tax increases that will cripple the economy.

INDEPENDENT MEDIA: Politician B only calls for tax increases on the top 5 percent of wage earners so that we might balance the budget.

POLITICIAN A (ad infinitum—oblivious to the facts): If you elect my opponent, Politician B, you will receive endless tax increases that will cripple the economy.

Comment: Politician A does not care about the truth of his assertion. In the example, his statement is false (as corroborated by the independent media). Instead, Politician A seeks merely to repeat his attack over and over again in order to take advantage of the psychological phenomenon that gives credence to repetition. Many repetitions of any assertion do not alter the truth of the assertion at all. Each is an independent event. This is a very common fallacy among politicians and advertisers.

The last three fallacies in this section primarily have to do with inductive argument. The reader is encouraged to refresh his or her memory of this type of argument by reviewing the presentation of induction in Chapter 5.

Hasty Generalization

This fallacy comes about when a generalization is formed from an atypical sample. Instead of properly following the rules of induction, the author considers the cases improperly. The practitioner of this fallacy can be said to "jump to conclusions."

Three of the most common reasons for doing so are: (a) the sample isn't large enough; (b) the sample isn't varied enough; and (c) the practitioner has been psychologically swayed.

Example Eight

Mr. Johnson concluded that Mrs. Smith would win the election for U.S. senator because most of his friends favored Mrs. Smith.

Comment: In this case, Mr. Johnson formed a generalization based upon an atypical sample; the sample is too small, and it is not varied enough. Thus, the conclusions may not be correct. There are, of course, times when a small sample causes no difficulty. If someone wanted to test the boiling point of water or the melting point of lead, a large number of tests would be unnecessary. For more on the correct procedure of induction, see Chapter 5.

Sometimes a person may be swayed even though the facts point otherwise. For example, Joan might acquire all the relevant information on buying a station wagon. As a result, she decides that the Ford wagon is the best. But later she demurs when a friend at work tells her that the Ford wagon *he* bought turned out to be a lemon. In this case Joan allows herself to be swayed from a sound judgment by the immediacy of the situation—a situation that represents an atypical case.

Improper Analogy

This fallacy results from improperly shifting grounds from properties belonging to one statement to those of another. Generally, the former is well-known, and the description beyond dispute. The latter is controversial. The use of the analogy represents an attempt to fix the character of the latter. For example, one might properly agree to the saying, "Where there's smoke, there's fire." This is generally a true statement. But even if one agrees to the saying, he or she might disagree with various applications of this, such as indicating that wrongdoing has occurred whenever there is a climate of negative innuendo.

Another example can be found in Plato's *Crito*. According to Plato, Socrates defended his acceptance of the state's punishment partly because he likened the state to his father. The reader in such an instance must decide whether analogy is fulfilling its proper role or is merely acting as a figure of speech to illustrate the author's point—which has no real logical content.

Incomplete Evidence

Often, we must make judgments without having all the possible evidence before us. This is a practical necessity. But sometimes this can lead us into error.

Example Nine

The president of the United States is not listed in the Washington, D.C., phone directory. Therefore, he must not have a private landline phone.

Comment: The Washington, D.C., phone directory is quite comprehensive, but it does not list the phone number of every private telephone. Some are unlisted. The inference in Example Nine is based upon incomplete evidence.

Shifting the Terms

In this second classification of logical fallacy the focus is on shifting the terms themselves in various ways so that what appears to be a tight inference really is not. It is an illusion created by *ambiguity* or by *false inference*. Each of these divisions, in turn, has three subclasses. As with shifting grounds, the best defense is to set out a clear outline and examine it closely.

Ambiguity

A. *Equivocation* creates ambiguity by using one term and assigning two different meanings to the term.

Example One

1. Madmen should be put in a nuthouse—(assertion)
2. My father often gets mad—(fact)

---

3. My father should be put in a nuthouse—(1, 2)

Example Two

1. The president controls a ballooning budget—(assertion)
2. Balloons are controlled by hot air—(fact)

---

3. The president is a bunch of hot air—(1, 2)

Comment: These arguments are not logically valid because in the first case the word *mad* is used in two senses. There is no logical connection between the two premises because there are no common terms by which an inference may be drawn.

The same is true of the two senses of *balloon* in the second case. Logical inference requires some common ground by which it may create a new proposition. (Mediate inference requires at least two premises; immediate inference requires only one.) In the above examples, this appears to be the case, but upon examination of the logical outline, it is seen not to be. In equivocation, ambiguity is created since multiple meanings legitimately exist. Unless the exact same meaning is maintained throughout, illogical conclusions may be drawn. To guard against possible equivocation, try substituting synonyms for the disputed terms and then test for validity.

B. *Amphiboly* creates two distinct meanings from a poorly formed grammatical structure.

Example Three

Those who ice fish often catch colds.

The stockbroker killed himself after an affectionate farewell from his fiancée with a shotgun.

Comment: In the first example it is unclear whether the word *often* attaches to *ice fish* or to *catch colds*. The sentence's meaning is different in the two cases.

The second sample is likewise caught between the two meanings implied by the dangling phrase *with a shotgun*. The effect is that the dangling phrase may attach to the manner of the stockbroker's death *or* to the manner of his affectionate farewell.

Though these above examples seem comic, the amphiboly can cause very serious effects. Documents released from World War II suggest that the Japanese sent a message that was an invitation to discuss surrender *before* our dropping of the atomic bomb. The message was misread due to amphiboly. Think how history has been changed due to this single instance of logical fallacy!

Proper grammatical structuring should alleviate this difficulty. When reformulating another's argument and two possibilities obtain, one should, by the principle of fairness, always choose the stronger interpretation.

C. *Accent* owes its multiple meanings to an unusual context. The sentence as literally read has one meaning, and the context creates another, unstated meaning. For example, if you wrote on an employee's work report, "Harris was sober today," you would not literally be saying anything harmful. But the context could be interpreted to mean that though Harris was sober today, on other days he was not.

Quoting out of context, or other alterations of the context, may create this fallacy. The way to uncover this difficulty is to outline it and supply the proper context as background conditions (perhaps via suppressed premises).

False Inferences

A. *False cause* occurs when there is no good evidence by which to infer a causal relationship. This may be the most dangerous of all the groups of fallacies, because it may appear to many to represent a proper inference. Part of the reason for this is that often one cannot isolate a general methodology that dictates it is always the case that such-and-such exercise of it is wrong. Compare these two instances from the following example:

Example Four

1. More students go to college today than in 1915, and the country is filled with more violence today

than in 1915. Therefore, sending young people to college causes a rise in violence.

2. Of all cocaine addicts, 98 percent started out drinking coffee before their drug use, and later they moved to cocaine. Therefore, drinking coffee leads to cocaine addiction.

Comment: These two selections operate on different principles. In the first selection the conclusion is justified by *post hoc ergo propter hoc* (after the fact, therefore because of the fact). This is an improper justification. Just because something happens after something else does not mean that a causal relationship has been established. Yet, the standard definition of cause as the constant conjunction of temporally contiguous events seems, structurally, to be very similar to the fallacy.

What is needed is *more* than knowing that one group of actions followed another group to assert causation. More cases need to be examined to determine whether or not a constant conjunction occurs. Such research would require all the controls of modern scientific method. Yet, even at that, there will be controversial cases such as the alleged cause-and-effect relationship between pornography and sexual violence.

In the second example, statistical correlation is the vehicle of inference. As with the first example, there are proper and improper usages of this principle. It was statistical correlation that established the link between cigarette smoking and cancer. This was a valid implementation of the technique, but it is obvious that such a method can easily be abused.

The best way to steer clear of failures from either of the above modes is to endeavor to connect the usage in question to some body of established scientific theory. Such a strategy is called *projection*. It dictates that one be able to project the unknown or disputed causal relationship into an entrenched paradigm. This amounts to finding the mechanisms and placing those mechanisms into an accepted common body of knowledge. In most cases such a projection works. However, when whole bodies of scientific knowledge change, it is useless (as with the change from Ptolemy to Copernicus in astronomy). But these cases are rare. In general, careful scrutiny and projection are one's best tools against false cause.

B. *Composition* is less intricate. This fallacy states that properties properly assigned to the *part* may also be assigned to the *whole*. For example, one could have very sturdy bricks (parts) and yet construct a very flimsy building (whole) with those bricks. In this case the whole has a different property than the individual parts have when they are examined separately.

C. *Division* is just the opposite of composition. This fallacy states that properties properly assigned to the *whole* may also be assigned to the *part*.

Example Five

1. The federal bureaucracy is inefficient—(assertion)
2. Joe works in the federal bureaucracy—(fact)

---

3. Joe is inefficient—(1, 2)

1. Lions are virtually extinct—(fact)
2. Simba is a young lion—(fact)

---

3. Simba is virtually extinct—(1, 2)

Comment: These examples both demonstrate that the individual does not necessarily share in the properties of the whole. It is perfectly coherent to have a very efficient Joe and a very healthy Simba. The whole and its properties may be of a different level of logical description than that of the part. This is because the class is a different logical type than the individual. When we ascribe properties to the class, we do so in a different way than when we ascribe properties to an individual—for example, no one would claim the *class* of redheaded men to be redheaded.

Untangling this relationship is too intricate for our present purpose and is an issue of dispute among philosophers of language. However, it is clear that in general the fallacy of division occurs when we examine nonessential traits and distribute them to each member. Thus, Joe is not a part of the federal bureaucracy by virtue of his being efficient or inefficient. The defining characteristic has to do with who pays his salary. Therefore, inefficiency is an accident and does not necessarily distribute among the members of the class. Likewise, being extinct is an accidental property of lions. Therefore, no necessary link can be made to one of the parts.

Much of this analysis applies to composition as well, except that in the case of the fallacy of composition, we are talking about a synonymy between the essential traits of the parts and those of the whole. Where there is no synonymy, or when the traits are accidental and not essential, the fallacy of composition may result.

Failure to distinguish these differences can lead to false inferences. Throughout, the student should familiarize him- or herself with logical fallacies as aids for creating correct evaluations.

The purpose of studying fallacy is that it might inform upon personal worldview to make it more critical of what is presented to it. We must treat presentations of argument with mitigated skepticism that is grounded in analytic tools that can point out where the problem lies. By understanding these relationships, we are empowered to be more critical readers and consumers of popular media. These skills help us to engage in the modification of the common body of knowledge.

The Common Body of Knowledge

We all live in communities. Each community accepts a common body of knowledge that defines how facts are understood and what values are to be endorsed. Because this concerns community and not the personal worldview, there will be by definition more diversity and compromise. This entails a range of necessary toleration.

The critical point for students of critical inquiry is how much toleration is enough and how much is too much. In the United States at the writing of this edition of the book, there is some dispute about how to teach secondary school biology concerning evolution. Virtually every single biologist, qua biologist, believes in one of the major theories of evolution. Each of these theories suggests that *Homo sapiens* came about through a process of gradual change that has a material account. For many in the Abrahamic religious traditions (Christians, Jews, and Muslims), this account differs from that of the book of *Genesis* (found in the Torah). This creationist account suggests that the world was created in six days (the seventh being a day of rest). On the face of it, these two accounts seem to be in variance; they appear to be logically inconsistent.

If you are a school district superintendent, what are you to say if your community demands that you (a) teach creationism instead of evolution, or (b) teach creationism alongside evolution? (For the purpose of this example remember that virtually 100 percent of all practicing biologists and graduate programs in biology believe in evolutionary theory and require facility in evolutionary theory in order to perform research.)

This is a real test of toleration. Clearly, from the practitioners' perspective evolution is the only theory to be taught in secondary school science classes. But what of the people who live in the school districts? In some cases they are the majority, and they demand either choice (a) or choice (b) above. Is truth a popularity contest? What about the rights of the sons and daughters of these creationist advocates who aspire to careers in biology or medicine?

This sort of question is an example of an important issue concerning toleration that the community must ask itself. In reality the actual playing out of this question will probably involve multiple communities: families, churches, synagogues, mosques, school districts, states, the scientific community, the nation, and so on. Wherever the question plays out, the issue of the common body of knowledge is crucial and requires social discussion.

The reason this is relevant to you, the developing critical reader, is that you need to understand how to think about social, political, and religious issues as you evaluate arguments. It is important to have these sensitivities and critical skills at your disposal as you engage in the hunt for truth.

Exercise

Access a source of news—newspaper, radio, television, or Internet home page—on an issue that is somewhat controversial within the community. Set out what you believe to be the community worldview conflicts at stake, and use your personal worldview standpoint to argue for where the limits of toleration should be.

Notes

1. This was a lynchpin of my friend, the late Roderick Chisholm. He held that there were normative duties to establishing sound, reliable epistemological procedures that might free us from error and enable us to embrace all that is true. See *Theory of Knowledge* (Englewood Cliffs, NJ: Prentice Hall, 1966). My own take on this issue is set out in *The Good, the True, and the Beautiful* (London and New York: Continuum, 2008), Chapters 4 and 5.

2. Michael Boylan, *A Just Society* (Lanham, MD, and Oxford: Rowman and Littlefield, 2004), 21.

3. *Contradictions* can be understood deductively or inductively. I am glossing quickly here. For a more complete treatment see Boylan, *A Just Society*, Chapter 2.

4. The exposition of these from this author's perspective are set out in *Basic Ethics*, 2nd ed. (Upper Saddle River, NJ: Prentice Hall, 2009), Part 2.

5. Boylan, *A Just Society*, Chapter 6.

CHAPTER 3

Confronting the Media

Many readers of this book are most often confronted with claims from the media, and so it is appropriate to set out a few examples of critical inquiry that move outside the traditional academic presentation mode. Because you are reading a book and cannot hit a button to start a YouTube sequence, I'll do the best I can with the media available to present edgy ads that make claims upon the observer.

Along this line, I will present three advertisements that make claims. Then, in the *comments* section, I will give examples of how to use the tools of critical inquiry introduced in this chapter to address some initial reactions to these ads and one example of how to apply them to phishing. Afterward, in the exercises section, you will be called upon to create similar reactions to the same sort of media input. This exercise will be repeated in Chapter 6 in order to add the skills involved in reconstruction of logical argument—both deductive and inductive.

In this chapter the focus will be on presenting the media depictions and teasing out possible critical inquiry stances (through personal and community worldviews).

The Media[1]

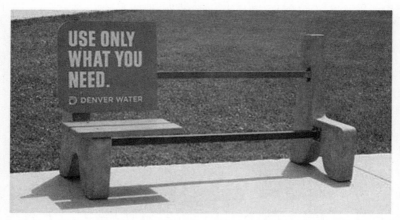

Comment: The point of contention is that we ought to drastically reduce water (the bench is two-thirds gone). The critical perspective is heightened by the oddness of seeing a park bench with only one-third there. If the picture is taken to be proportionally representative, then we should all reduce water consumption by two-thirds. The personal worldview that would be attracted to this would be one that purports an environmental conservation standpoint.

Those who think that the environment is ours to exploit in order to enhance the creation of personal wealth will object to this personal worldview standpoint. The common body of knowledge (one critical component of the shared community worldview) will view water conservation (in particular) and environmental protection (in general) as something that needs to be addressed individually or by public policy. These two approaches are different. Because only one person sits on a bench at a time, it would seem that the individual emphasis is what is being highlighted here. In this case it seems related to fulfilling real function (such as sitting on the bench) and nothing else (such as laying out your lunch or your briefcase). These amount to the dictum of using what you really need and not more.

It is important that the symbol presented is a bench. We think of a bench as a very basic public accommodation for those with weary limbs (just as water is also a basic boon for the thirsty).

Comment: This ad confronts the issue of how we regard people with HIV/AIDS. The point of view it elicits is rather sympathetic to the person in the bubble—presumably the person with HIV/AIDS. The critical perspective is heightened by the fact that none of us wants to live in a bubble separated from our community. We are social beings, so that discrimination hits us hard. None of us wishes to be relegated to the status of *the other*. Now there is still a fissure in the common body of knowledge about HIV/AIDS. Some say that those who contract the disease (for the most part) have engaged in illicit sex or intravenous drug use and do not deserve our compassion. But the ad confronts such hard-heartedness by depicting a young model who seems ready to enter into all that life has to give instead of dying. The ad seeks to confront the common body of knowledge position of those who wish to marginalize these souls who have contracted a fatal (treatable but not curable) disease.

Comment: This ad confronts the issue of the effects of smoking on public health. The bus is a public conveyance and so reinforces the message that smoking is not simply a personal matter but that it affects everyone. Just as the bus pollutes its gasses into the atmosphere, so does the smoker's behavior enter the public space. The common body of knowledge and the shared community worldview are appealed to here. The eradication of smoking and the eradication of polluting busses are linked. We all would agree that we are sickened by the latter, but does that also imply the former? Is this a fair analogy?

Phishing

Dear Maria,

Congratulations! You are the winner of a random Internet lottery that is sponsored by Fortune 500 companies to draw new interest in their products. For more information about your prize, click on the following link: http://www .internetwinners@Fortune500promotion.com.

Next screen:

Congratulations! In order to claim your prize of $100,000 you need to provide the following information:

Name:
Address:
Name of Bank:
Account Number:
Any Password:
Social Security Number:
(We are required under law to report your earnings to the Internal Revenue Service.)

Comment: The actor W. C. Fields used to say in his movies, "You can't cheat an honest man," even as he was playing a rogue who ran con games. Phishing (a form of spam intended to defraud) requires its respondents to believe that there is a gravy train a comin' round the bend and that Lady Luck will someday make their lives wonderful! This sort of personal worldview delusion makes gullible clients among small percent of the population. All the phishers need is a positive response from a few percentage points of the population that receives their spam message. Of course this is a hoax. Of course they can use the information you give them to access your bank accounts and take what little you might have there. This is a personally directed message, so the shared community worldview is not in play. However, the common body of knowledge maxim that Lady Luck is just around the corner and life can turn around again is a force behind this phony presentation. These personal worldview tenets, if examined critically, will be seen as irrational. Most recipients make this connection, but not all. It is that difference that can make these crooks rich.

Exercises

Use the tools of critical inquiry set out in this section (personal worldview, community worldview, and the common body of knowledge) in order to tease out what values and issues are at stake in the following four exercises on ads and phishing. Be sure to connect to the theoretical principles presented in this section.

Exercise 1

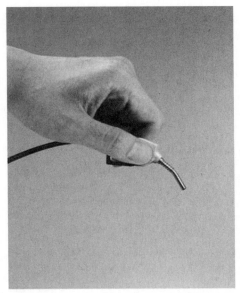

Exercise 2

Exercise 3

Exercise 4

Phishing Message

Dear Friend,

I am the lawyer for Suzy Nasouli, who was recently forced to leave the country but cannot get her money out. We need a third party who has an American bank account in order to transfer the funds, which total $34 million. This was money that came from the Nasouli family mining fortune. It would be terrible for this money to be lost and Ms. Nasouli to become destitute. I implore you to help us

avoid this disaster. To thank you for your help, I have been authorized to offer you $5 million as a fee. Please contact me at your earliest convenience: ABC@yahoo.com.
Yours truly,
Bagavier Tasman, Esq.
Attorney at Law

Notes

1. Source: http://justcreativedesign.com/2008/07/30/192 -of-the-best-smart-clever-creative-advertisements. Accessed November 1, 2008.

PART TWO

RECONSTRUCTING THE TEXT

CHAPTER 4

Outlining Deductive Logical Argument

There are two recognized argument types: *deductive argument*, in which the conclusion follows necessarily from the premises, and *inductive argument*, in which the conclusion follows contingently from the premises. The accepted terminology is that deductive arguments are *valid* if the acceptance of the premises necessarily entails the conclusion. In cases in which the premises are also assented to be true, then the entire argument is categorized as *sound*. Sound arguments should be accepted by all people (by virtue of the synonymy between agent and argument being rational).

Inductive arguments follow contingently (meaning that their conclusions leave some room for possible doubt—albeit in many cases very small). More on this is in the next chapter.

The next term to be explained is *outlining*. Outlining is a process by which the reader reconstructs the presentation of the premises so that they entail the conclusion. There are various ways this is presented in formal logic. For the purposes of this book, an informal system of logical entailment is presented with the end purpose of making the reader demonstrate his or her understanding of the mechanical presentation of the argument. This is a very technical chapter. Thus I will put key terms necessary for grasping these concepts in italics. If you make it through this chapter, you will be empowered to confront deductive logical argument wherever it confronts you with powerful tools of analysis.

Topical versus Logical Outlining

The method of logical analysis taught in this volume is that of *logical outlining*. A logical outline is different from the style of a *topical outline*, which is the outline most of us were taught. The topical outline provides a summary of all that occurs within a given passage. It is a condensed presentation that allows one to skim over the high points of a given work.

In contrast to a topical outline, the logical outline seeks only to present arguments and points of contention. Any other material, such as classificatory remarks and various enumerations, is omitted from the logical outline. For example, consider the contrasting outlines that can be constructed from the following passage:

What sort of person makes the best high-level manager? We all know that many kinds of people enter management. They range across the spectrum of human nature—from the timid, sniveling, and spineless to the aggressive, high-powered motivators. But surely, we all know that the future of our companies depends upon the quality of upper-level management. Therefore, it is appropriate to ask what quality is inherent in the best of these leaders of industry. In three words, it is that each is a "calculated risk-taker." This can easily be seen from the fact that initiating bold, new action, which is a top-level manager's job, involves taking risks. The policies of the past have to be reexamined and, if found wanting, then bold, new, risky paths must be explored. Obviously, though, one cannot go off willy-nilly. Some savvy and calculation are required, since these risk-takers are more often than not the winners at the end of the day. This is what has made American industry great, and it must continue if we are to remain strong.

Logical Outline

1. A high-level manager must be able to boldly lead a company away from policies of the past—(assertion)
2. To move away from policies of the past is to take a new direction—(fact)
3. Initiating bold, new directions involves taking risks—(fact)
4. High-level managers must be risk-takers—(1–3)
5. Calculated risk-taking is more successful than uncalculated risk-taking—(fact)
6. High-level managers must employ the most successful strategies open to them—(assertion)

7. High-level managers must be calculated risk-takers—
    (4, 5, 6)

Topical Outline

I. Types of Managers
    A. Timid
       1. Sniveling
       2. Spineless
    B. Aggressive
       1. High-powered
       2. Motivator
    C. Similar to cross sections of humanity
II. Future of Industry
    A. Lies with upper-level managers
    B. Quality managers make good companies
       1. Risk-takers
       2. Bold new action
       3. Reexamine policies of past
       4. Tempered with savvy and calculation
III. Past Success of American Industry
    A. Depends upon risk-taking managers
    B. Must continue for the future

Let us consider, in reverse order, some of the differences between the topical and logical outline and then highlight the strengths of each. The topical outline can give you a summary of what is contained within a book or lecture. By condensing the material, through the use of key words and phrases, the reader can recall the flow and order of the text. Such an outline might be useful for creating an encapsulated reconstruction or for boning up on a large amount of material at a glance. It is for this latter purpose that topical outlining is usually taught in grammar school.

The logical outline, in contrast, is not a summary. It is an exact reconstruction of the argument contained within a given passage. Some textual material is omitted. It does not use the *classification* found in logical outlines unless it is directly relevant to the argument at hand. Thus, in the above example, the classification into the two types of managers is not included.

Also omitted are various side remarks. In the above example the depictions of "sniveling," "spineless," "high-powered," and "motivator" are all side comments. The remarks on the future of American industry are also side comments, since these remarks are not accompanied by an appropriate argument.

What remains is an exact depiction of the internal structure of the sentences meant logically to persuade us to accept some point of contention. This outline admittedly misses certain parts of a passage; thus, it is not comprehensive. But it is a more detailed and useful tool for understanding an argument than the topical outline. If one wanted to formulate an objection to this argument, the topical outline would not afford the reader the same view of all the logical relationships among sentences that the logical argument does. For this reason the logical outline can be viewed as a specialized form of outlining. It has a precise mission. But if one wishes to be comprehensive in note-taking, then this form could be supplemented with a topical outline.

The Purpose of an Outline

However, inasmuch as many (if not most) books and articles seek to be persuasive rather than merely descriptive, the logical outline becomes the single most important form of reaction. It forces one to come to grips with exactly what is being said. We have all heard people say, "I know what the author is saying; it's just that I can't form an outline of it." This statement is misleading. What the speaker means is that he or she has a general, vague idea of what is going on in the passage. It is for this reason that an outline cannot be formed, since logical outlining requires more precision than he or she currently possesses. When the speaker claims an understanding of the text but is unable to outline it, he or she is really saying that more than C percent but less than A percent is understood (assuming a five-level scale with A being the highest). However, it is the contention of this book that unless one has acquired a mastery of a text of at least A percent, a sufficient level of competence has not been met. Therefore, one advantage of logical outlining is that it demands a higher level of understanding from the reader.

It has been my experience in the classroom that most students are searching for opportunities to work in depth and really master the material. Often, in an effort to be comprehensive and broad in scope, the student is burdened with so many pages of reading that all he or she can hope to achieve is C percent. This breeds not only frustration but an entire framework of mediocrity. There is a very limited benefit if most of one's courses require a surface, facile level of comprehension in exchange for large, survey quantities of processed material.

At the very least, people should be given the opportunity to work in a depth that encourages multiple readings and slow, painstaking interaction with the text. I suggest that in the beginning, you ask your instructor to flag the most important arguments *after* you have read them once (see Chapter 1). This will provide some further structure from which to create your outlines. As the course progresses, you will develop toward identifying the arguments yourself and creating your own reconstruction from these judgments. It is at this final stage that you can justifiably feel that you are getting the most out of the argumentative prose.

Fairness in Reconstruction

One final word must be added on fairness in reconstructing arguments. Often when encountering a logical argument, one is faced with what seems to be a very simple-minded mistake or superficial flaw. One response to this discovery is to pounce on it and use it to reject the entire argument. However, I think such an approach is not useful. This is because the author need merely make a slight alteration concerning the supposed flaw and the argument will be saved.

It is better to note the alleged error and then make the alteration yourself. In this way you are operating on the principle that you desire to evaluate the strongest version of the argument. Finding superficially weak interpretations is like finding "straw men" who are easy targets. It proves very little when one defeats a straw man. It is better to give the author every benefit of the doubt and view the case in the best possible light. We can state this principle of fairness as follows:

> Always reconstruct an argument in its strongest form, even if it requires correcting trivial errors (though these may be noted elsewhere).

An example of this might be derived from our earlier sample on the qualities of the high-level manager (see pages 76–77). Now it is possible that one might read this passage and find the following points to disagree with:

1. There are no timid, spineless managers.
2. Risk evaluation is a much more complicated field than the passage suggests.
3. More traits are needed in a successful manager than simply calculating risk-taking.

Much more could be said, of course, but these three reactions typify a large group of possible responses. Point 1 may be true, but what effect does an incorrect classification have on the argument's point of contention? None. This point can easily be conceded without weakening the argument at all. Therefore, under the principle of fairness outlined above, it would not be an appropriate avenue for evaluation. Point 2 may also be correct, but unless one could show that the simplification engaged in distorts the force of the normative background condition of which it is a part, then it will have no significant impact upon the conclusion.

The distinction in point 2 may be one of degrees. If this is the case, the student may feel some alteration of the premise is necessary. Under the principle of fairness, the student is obliged to do so after duly observing in a note that such a change is required to make the argument valid.

Finally, in point 3 we have a statement that does indeed affect the conclusion. If calculated risk-taking were intended as a sufficient condition for high-level management, then we would only have to go down to the racetrack to hire the next batch of senior-level officials. Rather, the student must make the charitable assumption that the author intends to highlight *necessary* rather than *sufficient* conditions.

By illustrating a necessary condition, the rhetorician only needs to show that the manager must have this particular trait. It says nothing about what else might be needed. To attack the writer because sufficient conditions have not been offered as well would be to require the writer to provide material beyond the purpose of the writing. This is surely unfair—unless you also wish to attack that purpose itself.

The reader of goodwill approaches a passage and decides that something important is missing. But then it must be judged whether the alleged error is one that is (a) really important to the conclusion, and (b) not able to be rectified by relatively minor means (such as assuming a necessary rather than a sufficient condition).

Such restrictions are important to observe, both out of fairness to the writer involved and to save one's attention for those parts of the argument that are essential to the view being put forth. For it is really this essential point of view that lies at the heart of the argument. Finding and zeroing in on it provides a much more productive use of one's efforts.

Reading Questions

1. What is a topical outline?
2. What is a logical outline?
3. When is it appropriate to use a logical outline, and when a topical outline?
4. How does logical outlining affect reading comprehension?
5. What is the "principle of fairness"? Why do we need it?

The Mechanics of Outlining

Now we are ready to go about the business of actually creating an outline of a deductive logical argument. Both the orders of logical presentation and genesis will be discussed. In addition, a few items of specialized interest are included at the end of the chapter. The student is encouraged to read the following example closely and then to refer to it while reading the rest of the chapter.

Editorial in the *Hometown Gazette*

Residents of fair Hometown, we've got a problem—a big problem. This problem must be addressed now! What I am talking about are *potholes*! Yes, you have seen them arise and

grow each spring when the winter thaw leaves its debris behind. At first they were only fissures, but now they threaten
road safety and the general condition of our automobiles. Do
you know what can happen to your car when you hit one of
those potholes at 40 miles per hour? Your axle gets bent out
of shape. And axles are expensive to replace. It's therefore
time for a change! The city needs to fix its potholes. Oh, I
know the mayor says there is no room in the city budget for
any more cost-cutting in order to fix potholes. And he's
right. The budget is tight as a drum. Therefore we must raise
taxes to pay for the repairs. We can't delay. Write His Honor
today. The city needs to raise taxes to fix those potholes!

Logical Outline

[1. The city's residents prize their automobiles' general condition and their own safety—(fact)]
2. There are many large potholes in the city—(fact)
3. Large potholes harm the condition of automobile
   axles as well as general driving safety—(fact)
4. The city needs to fill its potholes—(1–3)
5. The city is presently operating with a budget that
   cannot be trimmed—(assertion)
[6. Filling potholes costs money—(fact)]
[7. The only way a city can find money for a project is
   by cutting spending or by raising taxes—(assertion)]
8. The city can fix potholes only by raising taxes—
   (5–7)

---

9. The city needs to raise taxes to fix potholes—(4, 8)

Now let's pause a moment in order to see how one moves from text to outline.

Step One—As mentioned in Part One, the beginning of the process upon the second reading of a text is to try to discover what the principal point of contention is. In the editorial above, the point is to exhort the raising of taxes in order to fix potholes. This then becomes the conclusion of the argument. One must always begin an outline with the conclusion (more on this later).

Step Two—After the conclusion is established, a common technique is to analyze the conclusion in its component parts. In this case the conclusion has two parts: (a) the city needs to fix its potholes (the need), and (b) the city needs to raise taxes (the solution). If we were to create an argument with these two subconclusions, we'd be done.

Subconclusion: The city needs to fix its potholes.
Subconclusion: The city needs to raise taxes.
Conclusion: The city needs to raise taxes to fix its potholes—justification is subconclusion$_1$ and subconclusion$_2$

Step Three—After the subconclusions have been set out, the next step is to find the justification for each subconclusion. For example, in the first subconclusion the passage mentions all the potholes that have occurred in the city streets as a result of the difficult winter. These damage the citizens' cars. The text leaves it like that. However, a missing link exists: The citizens value safety and their cars' overall condition. This might seem commonplace, but without such a premise the first subconclusion could not be attained.

This requires the addition of a suppressed premise (enthymeme) (see Chapter 1). We place brackets around suppressed premises to show the reader that we understand that these have been added by the reader of the text in reconstruction in order to make the inference tighter. The result is as follows:

[1. The city's residents prize their automobiles' general condition and their own safety—(fact)]
2. There are many large potholes in the city—(fact)
3. Large potholes harm the condition of automobile axles as well as general driving safety—(fact)
4. The city needs to fill its potholes—(1–3) = subconclusion$_1$

A similar reconstruction can be made for the second subconclusion. At the end of the process, an argument should result that looks like the argument reconstruction presented above. This is a shorthand description of how to create a logical argument. In order to provide more details, we need to introduce additional terms in the context of those already set out.

Vocabulary for Reconstructing Deductive Logical Argument

(For other terms see also the glossary at the end of the book.)

Dividing the text. The text may be divided into three parts: argument, classification, and side comments.

Proposition. A declarative sentence with truth-value.

Premises. These are the building blocks of argument. The individual sentences of an argument are called premises. In the sample on page 85, the sentences numbered 1–8 are all premises. Collectively, the premises cause one to accept the point of contention; they logically imply the conclusion.

Conclusion. The point of contention. It is what the argument aims for. In the sample, sentence 9 is the conclusion. The justification of a conclusion is always an inference. A line (such as that under sentence 8) or three dots—∴—are used in logical outlines to set off the conclusion.

Argument. An argument consists of at least two sentences, one of which logically follows from the other. The statement said to follow is the conclusion and the supporting statement is the premise. The vehicle that allows one to move from premise to conclusion is called an inference. In this book we present arguments that generally consist of at least two premises since these are the most common arguments.

Therefore, the rules of argument put forth in this chapter will primarily be directed at these arguments. There are two broad classes of argument: inductive and deductive. Chapter 4 concentrates on deductive argument while inductive argument will be presented in Chapter 5.

Classification. This is one of the three divisions of the text. It is a mode of analysis in which classes are created on the basis of a division made in the common body of knowledge (see Introduction).

Side comments. This is another of the three divisions of the text. Anything that is not an argument or a classification will be labeled a side comment. This label does not imply that these comments are of no value. However, they are not the primary focus of this book.

Justification. A justification comes after a premise and is the proximate reason for accepting the premise. Three kinds of justification are used to aid in creating an evaluation. They have been divided in this way for their utility in constructing essays. The three types of justification are assertion, fact, and inference.

Assertion—This is the weakest justification. It means that the premise is true simply because one person has said it. The truth-content of the proposition involved may be doubted. In the above sample, premises 5 and 7 are supported by assertion.

Fact—This is the second strongest justification. It means that most listeners would accept the given truth put forth as objectively correct. When outlining historical texts, one should make reference to the beliefs of the time, such as "the Earth is the center of the universe," which might count as fact for speakers before the seventeenth century. In the above sample, premises 1, 2, 3, and 6 are justified as fact.

Inference—This is formally the strongest justification. It generally consists of at least two premises. (In some special cases one premise might count as an inferential justification in a deductive argument. This is called an immediate inference. Also, if you find that you have *more* than four premises listed as a justification, check your work! Chances are that you have compressed two inferences that should remain separate.)

The force of the inference arises from the combination of premises with our common sense. For example, if one accepts premises 1–3 in the sample, then he must also accept premise 4. Thus the justification for accepting premise 4 is simply our having accepted premises 1–3. When this connection is such that it cannot be doubted, the inference is called *tight*. When one can still doubt the inference, it is called *loose*. For example, in the argument, (a) dropping a water balloon from the second-story window causes the passerby to become wet, but (b) a water balloon was not dropped; therefore, (c) the passerby did not get wet (a, b), and the inference at (c) is loose because it can be doubted. It is possible the passerby got wet via another means, such as a rainstorm; thus, the inference at (c) is loose and unacceptable.

Suppressed premises (enthymemes). These are premises that are needed to make an inference but are not explicitly made by the writer. In the sample, premises 1, 6, and 7 are suppressed. To show their special status these premises are placed within brackets.

One important caution: When adding new premises, be sure the added material is in the spirit of the author's other positions; you would not want to add something that the original author would not have supported.

Interlocking premises. Interlocking premises refer to a property of an argument that obtains when all the premises are represented directly or indirectly in the conclusion's inference. In the sample there are eight premises. Premises 4 and 8 are found directly in the conclusion. Premises 1, 2, and 3 are found in premise 4. Since premise 4 is directly in the conclusion, 1, 2, and 3 are indirectly in the conclusion. Likewise, premises 5, 6, and 7 are found in 8, so that premises 5, 6, and 7 are also indirectly in the conclusion. Thus, in the sample all the premises are found directly or indirectly in the conclusion. This means that the sample argument possesses interlocking premises.

Valid argument. An argument is valid when all the inferences are tight and all the premises are interlocking. In a valid argument, if one were to accept all the premises, he or she would *have* to accept the conclusion. Be careful to observe that nothing is said here about the truth of the premises themselves. All that is asserted is that if we accept the premises, we must accept the conclusion. Thus, this argument, (a) all cats drink beer and (b) all beer drinkers are good bowlers; (c) all cats are good bowlers, is valid, though both its premises are false. But if we accept them, we must accept the conclusion. Thus we can see that validity is strictly a formal relationship between premises and conclusion. Understanding validity in this way will help with writing evaluations.

Sound argument. An argument is sound if it is valid and all its premises are true. Thus, in the example above about cats and bowling, though it is valid, it is unsound. When an argument is sound, we must accept the conclusion.

Chain argument (also called *sorites*). A chain argument occurs when the conclusion of one argument becomes a premise in a later argument. If we assume interlocking premises, then the truth of the chain argument depends upon the truth of all its constituents. The arguments thus become interdependent; their fates are tied together. Often sorites consist of a number of these arguments built into a long chain, all dependent upon each other. The whole is only as strong as its weakest link.

Concise Guide to Reading and Reconstructing Deductive Logical Argument

The Order of Logical Presentation Rules for Assessing Another's Argument

I. Finding the argument and outlining it
  A. Preliminary readings
    1. First reading. Define a section of text, such as a chapter, and read it rapidly. Don't stop. Don't take notes. Just read. Go quickly, almost skimming. After this reading, mark down the key points you remember.
    2. Second reading. With your sketchy first reading notes in front of you, go through the text again. This time, take a pencil and make a check in the

margin each time you feel an important point is being made. Read in your book at a normal pace. After you finish, go back and decide whether any of your checks can be combined with any others. Divide your text into sections according to these notations.

B. Outlining

　1. Titling and labeling. Take each section of text you have demarcated above and assign a title to that section. This title should reflect the point of the passage. Next to your title indicate whether this section of text is an argument, classification, or side comment.

　2. Argument reconstruction. Take all the sections that are arguments and compare titles. Combine any sections that are essentially identical. Then take one of the titles and concentrate on that portion of text. Your title will become the conclusion of the argument.

　　Next, determine what material in that passage might be used to logically support the conclusion. List these points. Put each statement into the form of a succinct proposition using your own words. Now set your text aside and try to combine the various propositions into inferences that eventually will cause your conclusion. You may have to add premises of your own creation in order to do this. Remember, all premises are to be in your own words. Bracket all suppressed premises (the ones you add). Once you have completed the reconstruction, you can test the argument for validity and soundness.

II. Testing for validity

A. Interlocking premises

1. Determine whether the proper argument has interlocking premises. If not, alter the argument so that it has interlocking premises (adding suppressed premises when necessary). To determine whether an argument has interlocking premises:

a. Begin (step one) with the conclusion and note which premises are directly present in the justification.

b. Next (step two), note which other premises are associated directly with those already noted as being in the conclusion. Follow this procedure again until all direct relationships are accounted for.

c. Finally (step three), make a list of all premises noted and compare this list with the numbers of premises. If they are identical, then there are interlocking premises.

2. From the sample: Step one shows that premises 4 and 8 are the justification of the conclusion. Step two shows that premises 1, 2, and 3 are directly in premise 4, and premises 5, 6, and 7 are directly in 8. Step three shows that the sum of direct and indirect premises tied to conclusion 1, 2, 3, 4, 5, 6, 7, 8 is equal to the premises of argu-

ment 1, 2, 3, 4, 5, 6, 7, 8, and the sample argument has interlocking premises.

B. Tight inferences

1. Determine whether the argument has tight inferences. If not, alter the argument so that the inferences are tight (adding suppressed premises when necessary).

2. To determine whether the argument has tight inferences, begin with the inference in the conclusion. Read the two to four premises used in the inferential justification. Then read the conclusion itself. Does the conclusion follow from those premises exactly? You may have to try this several times before you are sure.

3. Think critically: Is there any way you could accept those premises and *deny* the conclusion?[1] If there is, then the concluding inference is loose and must be corrected.

4. Next, repeat this procedure for each of the inferences found among the premises. In each case the inference must be tight. If you engage in any corrections, the entire process should be repeated lest your correction of one premise involves the weakening of another inference. For example, in the sample, first one would read premises 4 and 8 and then determine whether the conclusion must be accepted. Finding the answer positive, premises 5, 6, and 7 would be read to determine whether premise 8 must be accepted. Finally,

premises 1, 2, and 3 are read with premise 4. After going through this process, one can deduce that the inferences are tight.

C. Judgment of validity

After the premises have been found to be interlocking and tight, one may judge the argument valid.

III. Testing for soundness

After judging an argument to be valid, then examine:

A. Truth of premises

1. Assertions. Begin your investigation of the truth of the premises by examining those premises whose justification is an assertion. Since the assertion is the weakest form of justification, it is most probable that any disagreements will occur here. When you find a disagreement, list the general points you have against it in order to help you write an evaluation (see Part Three).

2. Facts. After surveying the assertions, determine whether you would wish to challenge any of the facts as being incorrect. Caution must be used when evaluating historical arguments. One cannot generally blame an historical audience for having accepted some scientific truism (such as the earth being the center of the universe). Any evaluation of an argument made by an historical figure should be charitable with respect to the "best available evidence."

3. Inferences. Since these have been checked for validity, no investigation is needed here.

B. Judgment of soundness

After completing steps one and two, one can conclude that all the premises are true. If they are, then because you've already judged it to be valid, the argument is sound.

IV. Testing for accuracy

A. After having set out the argument and tested it for validity and soundness, it is wise to return to the passage outlined. Have you captured the intention of the text? Are all additions to the argument in accord with the author's overall viewpoint? Has your wording of the premises been faithful to the meaning that the author intended?

B. If the answer to any of these questions is no, then you must return to the passage and make your corrections. Afterward, repeat items II, III, and IV.

V. Assessment of the argument

A. If the argument is judged to be valid, sound, and accurate, then the conclusion is termed true and must be accepted.

B. If it is found wanting in validity, then decide whether this can be rectified by some small change. The principle of fairness dictates that you make any changes that can save an argument's validity so long as (a) the change is not contrary to another position taken by the author, and (b) you duly note that you have made such a change to save the argument.

After completing items I–V, you are now prepared to begin an evaluation.

The Order of Logical Genesis Rules for
Creating Your Own Arguments

I. Begin with the conclusion
   A. Find out what you want to say. Your thoughts may be fuzzy.
   B. To aid in clarifying them, set down a thesis statement in the form of a succinct proposition.
II. Create a supporting argument
   This consists of the following four steps:
   A. Listing and titling. Make a list of all the reasons you believe support your thesis. When the list is complete, try to combine your various sentences into groups. Then assign a title to each group. The title should be in the form of a proposition.
   B. Inferential combinations. Next, formulate the other sentences in the group into propositions as well. At any point you may add or subtract further sentences. Finally, arrange your titles so that some kind of inferential arrangement exists among them. Remember, your overall goal is to prove your thesis.
   C. Finalizing the argument. Add or subtract various premises in order to formulate your argument. Keep in mind the rules for assessing the argument. The object here is to fine-tune your effort so that it conforms to the logical rules.
   D. Assessment. Assess your argument according to the manner prescribed in the order of logical presentation. When you find an error, correct and reassess the whole.

III. Review the final product

Congratulations, you have created a logical argument that may be used as a guide for constructing an entire essay. Each of the inferences in your supporting argument can count as a paragraph. The inference itself is the topic sentence for that paragraph. The supporting sentences in the inference become the body of the paragraph. Of course, an outline is the bare skeleton for your prose essay. Other sentences will be needed to create a smooth effect. These other elements might include classification for clarity and side comments that will expand and develop the point you are trying to get across.

Common Mistakes in Outlining Deductive Logical Arguments

1. Too many premises cited in one inference

It is a typical mistake for students to cite all the premises in the conclusion of the argument. This confutes the structure of subconclusions (described above).

2. Stilted sentences that do not really fit together

This is another common mistake. It is caused by students trying to stay so close to the text that they quote passages of the text in their outline. This is a problem. When you are outlining, you are *reconstructing* the text. Therefore, you should use your own words. By doing this, the inferences that you draw will follow from your own worldview and will be tighter. I would suggest that you should read around the passage containing the critical premises and then close the book (marking your place). Write down as many premises as you can. When you can think of no more or when you think you've lost your way, then reopen the book. Read the passage again. Then shut the book and give it another go.

3. Long premises

Many students create long premises that go on for several lines. These hyperpremises actually contain more than one premise and mar the atomic process of inference combination. Except for classification premises (which parse a topic into several parts and tend to be longer for that reason), try to make your premises read on one line as much as possible.

4. Weak inferences

Some students just mechanically create an inference every three or four premises without checking to be sure that the inference really follows. I believe this to be an artifact of haste. Be careful in setting out inferences. Make sure that when you read aloud the supporting premises to the inference, the subconclusion really is inferred in such a way that it cannot be doubted (the hallmark of deductive argument).

5. Improper mechanics

The last common error is when students leave out justifications. The whole process is about justifications. Without these, the outline is incomplete and will not be serviceable for creating a pro or con essay.

Appendix: Indirect Argument (Especially for Readers of Plato)

A special category of argument should be mentioned in this chapter—the indirect argument. This form of deductive argument varies from the stated form in one major way: Instead of having the point of contention proved positively, the logical complement is disproved or the possible choices are narrowed to one. Thus, indirect argument works in two ways: (a) through logical complements (*reductio ad absurdum*), or (b) through the principle of remainders.

Logical Complements (Reductio Ad Absurdum)

This type of argument works on a very simple principle: If you want to prove a point, first assume its opposite and then show how that opposite leads into an absurd (false) state of affairs. Since the opposite leads to an obvious falsity, the original point must be correct.

Example

"Very good, Cephalus," I said. "But what is the definition of Justice? Is it to tell the truth and to pay your debts? No more? And is this definition even correct? Suppose a friend deposits his weapons with me. When he did this he was perfectly in control. Later, when he is mad he asks for them back. Should I give them to him? Nobody would sanction this or call such an action right any more than they would require me to always speak the truth to my mad friend."

"This is true," he said.

"But then we were not right to say that Justice is telling the truth and repaying that which had been previously given."

PLATO, *REPUBLIC* I, 331C1–D3[2]

Thesis: Justice ≠ speaking the truth and paying one's debts.

Assume Antithesis: Justice = speaking the truth and paying one's debts.

Antithesis leads to Absurdity: One should provide a madman with weapons.

∴. Therefore, antithesis is wrong and thesis is proven.

Comment: Notice that this method relies on there being two and only two logical states, true and false, and that if an antithesis is shown to be absurd (false), then its opposite, the thesis, must be true. This relationship between sentences is called contradictory opposites.

It is important to sharpen one's understanding of opposites since this relationship is crucial for the operation of *reductio ad absurdum.*

The Four Propositions

"All swans are white" means "Everything that is a swan is also white."

"No swans are white" means "Nothing that is a swan is also white."

"Some swans are white" means "There is at least one swan that is white."

"Some swans are not white" means "There is at least one swan that is not white."

These may be combined as shown in Figure 4.1, where the sentences marked A and O and those marked E and I are contradictory opposites. These are the only relationships from which, in every case, one can immediately deduce the truth-value of one statement from that of another.

In the example on page 102, the *thesis* could be rewritten as an O statement: "Some cases of telling the truth and paying one's debts *are not* cases of justice." The corresponding *antithesis* could be written as an A statement: "All cases of telling the truth and paying one's debts are cases of justice." By showing the latter is false, we *have* shown the former to be true.

Caution on reductio *arguments.* The major caution here is that one is actually dealing in contradictory opposites. These are sentences whose complements have opposite truth-values. However, there is another brand of opposites, *contrary* or *polar* opposites, which have a different logical relation.

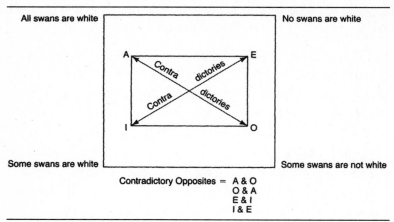

Figure 4.1: Contradictory Opposites

Contrary opposites may both be false. In other words, proving one false does not entail the other is true. For example, take these two sentences: All the sales associates in Johnson's Realty are in the Million-Dollar Club. None of the sales associates in Johnson's Realty are in the Million-Dollar Club. If only one-third of the sales associates in this company are actually in the Million-Dollar Club, then both the above propositions are false. Thus, proving one to be false does not entail the other being true. We can, therefore, conclude that A and E statements are not contradictory opposites since both may be false. Instead, they are called contrary opposites.

Likewise, if we compare an I and O proposition (see Figure 4.1) we have: Some of the sales associates in Johnson's Realty are in the Million-Dollar Club, and Some of the sales associates in Johnson's Realty are not in the Million-Dollar Club. Proving one of these statements true does not prove the other false. They may both be true if at least one member (but not all) of Johnson's Realty is a member of the Million-Dollar Club. We can therefore conclude that I and O statements are not contradictory opposites since both may be true. Instead, these are called subcontrary opposites.

Reductio ad absurdum only works when the thesis and antithesis are related as contradictory opposites. When this relationship exists, indirect argument by logical complements can be a powerful tool of persuasion.

Exercises on Contradictory Opposites

Directions: In the following, state whether the thesis and the antithesis are contradictory opposites. Write "yes" for contradictory opposites and "no" for any other relationship.

1. All first basemen are left-handed. No first basemen are left-handed.
2. Lake Michigan bass are not edible. No fish from Lake Michigan are edible.
3. Sam Jones and Martha Smith are corrupt politicians. No politicians are corrupt.
4. All red wine tastes better with meat. Gallo red wines don't taste better with meat.
5. All Hall of Fame frisbee players are still alive. Margo Washington is a Hall of Fame frisbee player who is still alive.

Remainders

The principle of indirect argument assumes a limited number of possible cases. You can show one to be the case if the others are shown not to be the case. The remainder is thus alone at the end and must be true. The group to be examined is conveyed by the thesis statement.

1. Someone in the group of three students who stayed late after school—Tom, Sue, or Bill—put a wormy apple on the teacher's desk—(thesis)
2. The apple was observed by the teacher at 3:45, immediately upon her return after a ten-minute absence from the classroom—(fact)
3. Tom was in the principal's office from 3:30 to 3:50—(fact)
4. Tom did not do it—(2, 3)
5. Bill had chalk dust all over his fingers since 3:00—(fact)
6. There is no sink in the room in which to wash up—(fact)
7. Bill did not leave the classroom—(fact)
8. No chalk dust was found on the apple—(fact)
9. Bill did not leave the apple—(5–8)

---

10. Sue left the apple—(1, 4, 9)

As you can see, this form of indirect argument relies heavily upon the initial group chosen. If it is wrong that someone in the group left the apple, then the final conclusion is skewed. For example, if someone sneaked in and left the apple, the conclusion would be false. This is, nonetheless, a very popular form of logical deduction. As long as you keep in mind the indefinite nature of the thesis statement, you may proceed accordingly.

Exercises on Indirect Argument

Directions: In the selections below, find the thesis that is proven. Then state briefly how the proof worked.

1. "Clearly," began the detective as he chomped down on his cigar, "one of the people in this house last night committed the murder—John, Mary, or Sally. The murderer's only access to the victim was via the dumbwaiter. John is too fat to fit into it, and Sally was too drunk to operate the intricate pulley system. Therefore, Mary is the murderer!"

2. Senator Jones's proposal of a completely flat tax rate with no exemptions or exceptions must be rejected. This is easy to demonstrate. Suppose we go along with the senator for a moment. Why does he advocate this flat tax? He says that it is because he wants to create a tax equally fair for all. Everyone believes that only a fair tax deserves to be passed. But how does a completely flat tax do this? "Equally fair" must mean that everyone bears an equal tax burden. That is, the impact of the tax on a person's life

should be the same no matter what his or her income is. But I put it to you that 20 percent taken from a poor man deprives him of rent money or food for his children, while 20 percent from a rich man merely affects his investment options. Since rent and food are more basic to survival than types of investments, the poor man accepts a heavier burden when taxes are all of one rate. This, according to our definition, is unfair. A completely flat tax rate is thus unfair.

Reading Questions

1. What are the interlocking premises?
2. What are tight inferences?
3. How do we judge an argument to be valid? Sound?
4. What is meant by a test for accuracy?
5. Briefly state the rules for creating your own argument.

Notes

1. This does not apply to inductive arguments.
2. All translations are by the author.

CHAPTER 5

Outlining Inductive Argument

The second sort of logical argument is inductive argument. To better understand what this is, let us first go further into what makes inductive arguments distinctive and then go through the techniques necessary for logical outlining of inductive arguments.

Example One

A.
1. All people are mortal—(fact)
2. Sally is a person—(fact)

---

3. Sally is mortal—(1, 2)

B.
1. Every person on historical record has died within 200 years of his or her birth—(fact)
2. Sally is a person—(fact)

---

3. Sally is mortal—(1, 2)

Comment: The difference between the above arguments is not so much the presentation of the inductive investigations as it is the manner by which the conclusion follows from the premises. In example A the conclusion follows *necessarily*. If the premises are true (and the inferences valid), the conclusion will also be true. In example B the conclusion follows *contingently*. It is still possible for the conclusion to be false even if the premises are true.

Two things can be said about this difference: (a) Deductive inference makes explicit mediate relationships already present, and (b) inductive inference goes *beyond* that which is present and points to something new. This something new is either a *generalization* or a *causal relationship*. These two features will be the focus of this chapter.

Generalization

Enumeration and analogy are two of the most common methods by which generalizations may be formed. When employed correctly, they are indispensable tools for inquiry. When utilized improperly, they lead us into error. In proper generalization, broad statements are created from a sample that is comprehensive. This means that the sample is large and varied enough to generate the general conclusion. In addition, the practitioner must be a dispassionate observer so as not to bias the findings.

Jointly, enumeration and analogy help to ensure a proper generalization. Let's look a little more closely at these two means of forming a generalization. Throughout this discussion, pay careful attention to the place of the common body of knowledge. Often it is the status of these background conditions that can make the difference between a good and bad argument (see also Chapter 2 on logical fallacy). Let's look a little more closely at these two means to forming a generalization.

Enumeration

In enumerative induction the strategy is first to list all the observed properties of something with the objective of making a generalization about that type of thing. Then one draws a conclusion about all members of the class from premises that are about the observed members.

Example Two

After listing all the physical traits of thirty people who successfully survived the malaria outbreak, it was found that all of them had sickle-shaped red blood cells.

All people with sickle-shaped red blood cells will be more successful in surviving exposure to malaria.

Logical Outline

1. A comprehensive list of physical traits of thirty people after an outbreak of malaria showed that these people shared the common characteristic of having sickle-shaped red blood cells—(fact)
2. These thirty people were the survivors among a larger group exposed to malaria—(fact)

---

3. Anyone with sickle-shaped red blood cells will be more successful in surviving exposure to malaria—(1, 2)

Comment: Enumeration is one device that enables one to create generalizations. However, it is clear that problems can occur. If the evidence presented in the examination is not exhaustive, or if the case under examination is typical, then one is likely to make a mistake (see the fallacy of incomplete evidence). For example, it might be true that most of the Nobel Prize winners of the 1980s were European or American, but that does not make Bishop Tutu of South Africa into a European or an American.

Though enumerative induction is imperfect, we can try to minimize our chances of error by making sure the sample is sufficiently large and varied and that the researcher is unbiased. By keeping these conditions in mind, we increase our odds for success.

Analogy

This is a common and productive form of inductive reasoning. Analogy rests on the assumption that objects that are similar in certain respects will be similar in other respects as well.

Example Three

1. When rats are fed food that has been seasoned with large amounts of salt, they die much sooner than the control group—(fact)
2. Humans and rats have certain physiological similarities—(fact)

---

3. Salt must lower the life expectancy of humans too—(1, 2)

Comment: The move from rats to humans is based upon an assumption that both species have digestive similarities that make experiments on one species apply to the other as well. This means that the similarities focused upon in the example are relevant. The presence of this common physiological system increases the chances that the other will also experience the effect experienced by one. This is where one must be careful. Obviously, there are instances in which the similarity is not relevant and there is no connection between the common trait and the new generalization that is sought. The two may be somewhat independent. For example, Joe may have won the raffle twice while wearing his red flannel shirt. This does not mean that wearing the red flannel shirt a third time has anything to do with winning the raffle a third time. The analogy is improper.

For analogy to be effective there must be some connection between the two traits such that the possession of the first increases the probability of the second. This increase must, itself, be the consequence of some mechanism (at least in principle).

To understand whether such mechanisms exist requires reference to the common body of knowledge (see Introduction and Chapter 2). This enables us to see how the generalization created in the conclusion fits with other information (such as the body of accepted scientific knowledge that we already possess). For example, if the new conclusion is in contradiction to, or is inconsistent with, the common body of knowledge, then one might have some doubt about the generalization. If it *is* correct, then we will need more than just a generalization to back us up. This further support will come from the concept of causation.

Causation

Within our common body of knowledge there are a great many causal connections that we make via this form of induction. These come about through an intricate mental mechanism that includes our memories of certain occurrences that are constantly conjoined with others. This can work from cause to effect or from effect to cause.

Example Four

A.

1. The clouds are darkening—(fact)
2. The wind is picking up—(fact)
3. There's a funny sensation in the air—(fact)

---

4. It is going to rain—(1, 3)

B.

1. The ground is soggy—(fact)
2. There are pools of water everywhere—(fact)

---

3. It must have rained—(1, 2)

Comment: In example A we are presented with circumstances that generally indicate that it is going to rain. This is an inference from cause to effect. The argument makes a *prediction* about the future. It assumes that these are circumstances that belong within the causal mechanism of a rainstorm. The high humidity and the rapid shift in atmospheric pressure are signified by darkening clouds, windy conditions, and an inexplicable sensation that comes through our skin, which acts as a quasi-barometer. It is important that these circumstances are observed as preceding the effect and that they are part of an overall structure that would scientifically sanction such causal links. If such a structure is not there, then either (a) the effect was not *caused* by the preceding conditions, but merely illustrates an accident or coincidence;

or (b) there is an underlying causal mechanism that science has not observed.

Conviction in possibility has led to many discoveries in the history of science. Scientists have vowed to search for and explain new networks of relations that would justify tagging their observed regularity as causal. Until they are provided, however, such ascriptions are merely unproven hypotheses.

The same holds true when you move from effect to cause. These are really just two ways of looking at the same process. This process defines a close relationship between premises and conclusion (cause and effect). The nature of this connection is sometimes as a *necessary condition*. For example, oxygen is a necessary ingredient to fire. It is impossible to have a fire without it. Thus, in one sense, oxygen can be thought of as a cause of the fire. However, there is another sense of cause as a *sufficient condition*. One may have oxygen and still not have a fire. Other conditions are also necessary—such as fuel and a threshold temperature. Together, these are both necessary and sufficient.

> *Necessary Condition:* Without the presence of a certain condition some specified effect will not occur.
> *Sufficient Condition:* With the addition of that condition some specified effect will occur.

Sometimes there are conditions that are sufficient and not necessary. To start a fire it is sufficient to have a lighted match and a dry newspaper. But these are not necessary for fire because it is possible to create a fire via other means.

Try making a list of examples that present cases of (a) a necessary condition, (b) a sufficient condition, and (c) joint necessary and sufficient conditions. These important concepts require a little work for you to become more familiar with them.

Another aspect of cause concerns the proximity of cause to effect. In a chain of events, something far removed is less likely to be fully responsible than something closer. (A close relation will be called a "proximate cause" and a distant relation will be called a "remote cause.") This is because, in the case of a remote cause, there are more intervening factors that, by themselves, bear responsibility for what happens.

Example Five

A. John thoughtlessly throws a cigarette butt on the dry leaves as he hikes on the trail. The leaves catch fire and the forest burns down.

B. John thoughtlessly throws a cigarette butt on the dry leaves as he hikes on the trail. The ash is about to die out when it is fanned by Mary, who keeps it alive and pours gasoline around the surrounding area. The fire grows and the forest burns down.[1]

Comment: In example A, John is the responsible cause of the fire because he is the proximate cause. His action directly brings about the forest fire. He is responsible and is therefore the cause. When we focus on who is to blame, we look to John.

In example B it is Mary who replaces John as the proximate cause. John's actions are still wrong (via contributory negligence). He is still part of the causal chain that causes the fire. But now John shifts from being the proximate cause to being the remote cause, for if Mary had not been there (in example B), no fire would have happened. It is Mary's action that directly brings about the forest fire. She is responsible as the primary cause. When we focus on who is to blame, we look primarily to Mary. (John is still somewhat responsible as a remote cause via contributory negligence.)

Proximate causes may be the most helpful part of the scheme for understanding *why* something happened. But remote causes are also useful. They contribute to our understanding of the larger context of *how* some effect came about.

Obviously, causal relations are a very important part of induction. Improper application of this form of induction can result in the fallacy of false cause (see Chapter 2). Thus, there is need for a method to aid the practitioner in establishing general causal relations. One such group of rules was set out by the English philosopher John Stuart Mill. Mill offered five methods.[2]

The first is called the *method of agreement*. By this method you look for examples of the given effect on a wide variety of incidents. Then you try to find the element common to each incident.

When an unusual pneumonia-like disease killed a number of American legionnaires in Philadelphia several decades ago, physicians were at a loss to discover the source of the germs and the vehicle of their distribution. Through careful use of the method of agreement in disparate cases around the world, British doctors discovered that old air-conditioning systems were a common element. From there it was discovered that excess water from the air-conditioning units had stagnated and created a perfect environment for these deadly microbes to grow and disperse.

By examining what was common to all the cases, the mystery was solved. Of course, this method can be abused, as in the following:

BARTENDER: Hey Joe, you're drinking quite a bit tonight.

JOE: I'm conducting an experiment.

BARTENDER: Oh yeah, how's that?

JOE: I'm always getting drunk, so I'm trying to find out why.

BARTENDER: What are your results?

JOE: Well, I've had bourbon and soda, rye and soda, and scotch and soda. Now I'm drunk. The only common element among the group is the soda. Next time, I'll cut out the soda![3]

Comment: In order to work correctly, one must make some preliminary assumptions about the agents involved. In this case a description of what might count as a relevant similarity or difference is in order. With these cautions in mind, the method of agreement can be a powerful tool in discussing causal connections.

The second of Mill's methods is the *method of difference*. In this case one item is eliminated from the environment, and it is then determined whether the effect is still manifested.

This technique is often used in treating asthmatics. Asthma is a breathing disorder often triggered by allergens (particles that create an allergic reaction). The traditional method of identifying the allergens responsible is to eliminate elements from the patient's life one by one. Each week, some item, such as chocolate, peaches, or feather pillows, is taken away. After the item has been removed, the patient's condition is carefully monitored. If symptoms subside, then there is a good chance that the eliminated item is an offending allergen.

Again, care must be taken that when one removes an item, it is really a single unit. Otherwise we might mistake the real causal factor. For example, one asthmatic might have her mattress removed and, as a result, improve. This does not necessarily mean that the patient is allergic to the mattress itself. It is quite possible that microscopic mites that live atop all mattresses might be the offenders. If this were true, one would not have to eliminate the mattress, but merely shield the patient with a plastic mattress cover to eliminate the allergen. Since our world is filled with interdependent collections of organisms, it is often difficult to be sure one is able to correctly follow the method of difference. This is because of the difficulty of removing one, and only one, variable (and keeping all external factors constant). But with careful attention to these possibilities some errors may be avoided.

The third method is called the *joint method of agreement and difference*. This is, just as the title suggests, a combination of the preceding two. By this procedure a much more sophisticated method is created that comes closer to the way we actually solve problems.

Using our example of the asthmatic again, we can illustrate the joint method as follows:

Example Six

Table 5.1: Joint Method

AGREEMENT		DIFFERENCE	
CONDITION	REACTION	CONDITION	REACTION
Regular foods, stuffed animals, uncovered mattress	Asthma	Covered mattress, regular foods, stuffed animals	No asthma
Special diet, stuffed animals, uncovered mattress	Asthma	Special diet, stuffed animals, uncovered mattress	Asthma
Regular foods, no stuffed animals, uncovered mattress	Asthma	No stuffed animals regular foods, uncovered mattress	Asthma

Comment: The joint method seeks to bring forth the necessary and sufficient conditions that are the result of employing each separate procedure. Together, they would provide a much richer sense of cause. The joint method eliminates those sufficient conditions that are not also necessary. Obviously, the problems outlined in the practice of each method are also to be repeated here. Further, it should be stated that though the ideal is to provide necessary and sufficient conditions, these cannot be guaranteed. As in any inductive argument, the conclusions are only contingent—not only in their inherent logical status, but also because they are relative to the thoroughness of the practitioner. This last point is of no small importance. Much of the recent controversy in cancer and AIDS research has hinged upon the propriety and utility of various research strategies about which there is much disagreement.

The next method is that of *residues*. This is similar to the argument by remainders found in Chapter 4. When one finds that a predicted result of known causes does not account for some phenomenon (*explanandum*), then it is probable that some new unknown factor is the cause (since the known factors have been exhausted). What would therefore remain might very well be the explanation (*explanans*).

This has happened in the history of science (and is happening now). The discovery of the planet Neptune occurred after Bouvard de Paris in 1821 published tables on the motions of the planets based upon Newtonian mechanics.[4] In 1845 a young aspiring scientist named Leverrier found problems with the calculations. Though they were mostly correct, there was a slight variation that could not be squared with observation. The only explanation that might right the issue would be the existence of a planet (as yet unobserved). This led to the discovery of Neptune. Thus, when all existing accounts are not sufficient to explain observational anomalies, the method of residues calls for finding either a new variable or an entirely new theory to explain things.[5]

A contemporary example of residues concerns the apparent discrepancy between the amount of observed matter in the universe (expanded analogically over the observed domain) and the theoretical prediction of the same by Einstein as modified by Hawking. This has led some scientists to modifications of the theory using a multidimensional approach (commonly known as string theory), while others want to create an entirely new structure (commonly known as loop quantum theory).[6] In each case the reaction is one akin to Mill's residues approach.

The last method to be mentioned is that of *concomitant variation*. This method differs from the joint method and its thesis that we can totally eliminate various elements from our experimental model. Such elimination is not always possible. For example, if we wanted to study the causal relationship between sunspots and the concentrations of certain types of radiation in the world, then clearly the joint method would be inapplicable. We cannot eliminate sunspots. What we can do is measure the variation of radiation levels whenever sunspot activity increases or decreases. Concomitant variation seeks to show that two conditions are causally related, since the variation of one leads to the variation of the other.

This method has been a powerful tool in science. Though it cannot provide necessary or sufficient conditions, it *has* been useful in discovering important causal connections between smoking and cancer, asbestos and asbestosis, sodium levels and arteriosclerosis, and so on.

Of course there is a danger that one might observe accidental correlations and from these incorrectly project a causal relationship where none exists. An example might be the asserted connection among drug addicts, homosexuals, and carriers of AIDS. Though drug addicts and homosexuals statistically have a much higher incidence of being infected than the general population, there is no essential connection among being a drug addict, a homosexual, and an AIDS victim. One becomes infected with the HIV/AIDS virus via the transfer of body fluids. This is the mode of transmission, *not* membership in some particular group. Thus, a celibate homosexual or a drug addict who always uses a clean needle would be at no risk of being infected. One must not mistake the *proximate* cause with a *remote* cause even if statistics seem to correlate equally with both groups.

Since necessary and sufficient conditions are not demonstrated, there is much room for dispute about how these correlations are to be analyzed and interpreted. There is always the risk of asserting the existence of a cause where none exists.

Special Hints for Outlining
Inductive Arguments

Inductive arguments can be outlined according to the general suggestions for outlining deductive arguments described in Chapter 4. The major difference between inductive and deductive arguments is that the conclusion of the latter is necessary and that of the former, contingent. This is also reflected in the way we check an inductive argument to determine whether it is a good one.

In the last chapter the criteria for a good deductive argument were presented. A deductive argument is good when it is *sound*. Soundness was defined as a valid argument whose premises are true. An inductive argument is good when it is *cogent*. Cogency is defined as: All inferences are highly probable (strong), and all premises are true.

Criteria for Good Arguments

Sound Deductive Arguments

1. Valid inferences
2. All premises true

Cogent Inductive Arguments

1. Strong inferences
2. All premises true

Amendments to the Order of Logical Presentation (set out in Chapter 4)

I. Find and outline the argument (as stated in Chapter 4)
II. Test for cogency (in the case of inductive arguments)
   A. Strong inferences. Do all inductive inferences seem highly probable? Go over the fallacies for induction presented in Chapter 2. Are the fallacies of hasty generalization, improper analogy, incomplete evidence, or false cause present? Is there anything else about the inductive inference that would cause you to doubt that it is usually true? If doubts are found, then you may use these as a basis for writing your evaluation. Double-check these with the rules governing *generalization* and *causation*.

B. Are all the premises true? Go over the premises justified as fact or assertion. If questions about the truth of these can be raised, and the premise cannot be restated to make it true (according to the principle of fairness), then these questions should be addressed in the argument evaluation. Double-check these with the rules governing *generalization* and *causation*.

III. Judgment of cogency

If, after completing the test for cogency, one can conclude that the inferences are strong and the premises are true, then the inductive argument is cogent and its conclusions should be generally accepted.

For the rest of the process of outlining, continue according to the instructions described in Chapter 4.

Exercises

Directions: Identify the arguments that are inductive and those that are deductive.

Group A

1. Sluggo, Rocky, and Bruiser are all successful boxers. They can take a punch—and still continue fighting. Therefore, successful boxers have to be able to take a punch.

2. All viruses are distinguished by being a single strand of RNA covered with a protein coat. This unknown

organism before us is simply a single strand of RNA covered by a protein coat. This unknown organism is a virus.

3. Most societies have sanctions against murder. The Hopi constitute a small society. The Hopi have a sanction against murder.

4. The gears on my automobile do not disengage easily. There is a popping noise occasionally when I depress the clutch. Pretty soon my clutch cable is going to break.

5. Whenever it rains, all hydrophobic organisms stay under cover. Right now it's raining. Let's go out and enjoy ourselves. There's no chance of getting rabies today.

Group B

1. Edward Jenner noted that Sarah Portlock, Mary Barge, Elizabeth Wynne, Simon Nichols, Joseph Merret, and William Rodway had all suffered cowpox, and they seemed not to be infected by smallpox in cases he might have expected it. To be sure, he inoculated them with smallpox directly. Nothing happened. Years passed and he repeated his observation. These people were immune. Jenner concluded that it was the cowpox that made them immune.

2. Yellow fever is an acute infection that creates a deeply jaundiced condition. Other symptoms include dizziness, rapid onset of fever, headache, nausea, and vomiting. Death may occur on the sixth or

seventh day of illness and has been known to occur in as many as 50 percent of those infected. During the Spanish-American War, Walter Reed was sent to Cuba to solve the problem. Reed narrowed the correlative antecedents from a large to a small list. The possible candidates for the cause of yellow fever were (a) mosquitoes who had fed on infected victims, (b) excreta of yellow fever patients, (c) dishes and silver of patients, and (d) clothing of patients. Reed built a mosquito-proof building and divided the interior space in two. One space contained mosquitoes who had fed on yellow fever victims. The other space was left alone. Non-immune volunteers were put in each half of the building. Volunteers on the mosquito side contracted the disease.

Next, the other items on the list were given to volunteers in a similarly constructed setting. One by one, and then in concert, these other factors failed to bring on the illness. Thus, by breaking up the list and eliminating each factor one by one, it was determined that mosquitoes alone transmitted the disease.

Arguments of Cogency

Directions: In the following exercises, decide which of these inductive arguments are cogent and why.

1. It is election night and Mrs. Johnson is ahead with 50 percent of the vote reported. Mrs. Johnson is sure to be elected.

2. My horoscope is usually right. Today it says I should be prepared to take financial risks. Therefore, I withdrew all the money from my bank account and am waiting.

3. In the months after our cat died, I suddenly realized that the indoor plants—which had always been scrawny—were now blooming in health. Nothing else in our apartment had changed. I'll bet our cat bothered them by eating leaves and scratching the stems.

4. The army trains its soldiers well in boot camp. Thus, these soldiers are ready for everything real war has to dish out.

5. "The only one who could have committed the murder is the person who had access to the murder weapon, had a motive, and was near the room where the crime was committed. You did it, Professor Plum! You killed Colonel Mustard with a lead pipe in the study." (Imaginary detective solving his case)

Reading Questions

1. What is enumerative induction?
2. What is induction by analogy?
3. What is the difference between necessary and sufficient conditions?
4. State the five methods of Mill.
5. What are the criteria for good deductive and inductive arguments?

Notes

1. These examples are adapted from those given by H.L.A. Hart and Tony Honoré, *Causation in the Law* (Oxford: Clarendon Press, 1959), 292–296, 358–361.

2. John Stuart Mill, *A System of Logic* (London: John W. Parker, 1843).

3. Adapted from an example given by Wesley Salmon, *Logic* (Englewood Cliffs, NJ: Prentice-Hall, 1963), 112.

4. For a further account see Edward Arthur Fath, *The Elements of Astronomy* (New York: McGraw-Hill, 1926), 170.

5. This was the case in Copernican astronomy, which replaced the Ptolemaic-based system. For an excellent account see Thomas S. Kuhn, *The Copernican Revolution* (Cambridge, MA: Harvard University Press, 1957).

6. Jan Ambjørn, Jerzy Jurkiewicz, and Renate Loll, "The Self-Organizing Quantum Universe," *Scientific American* 299, no. 1 (July 2008): 42–49.

Confronting Media in Reconstruction

Because many readers of this book are confronted with claims more often directed at them via the media than they are with claims from argumentative texts (philosophy, literature, history, business, and the like), I think that it is appropriate to create a very selective sample of visual advertisements and one common phishing letter that will extend these principles to other areas of readers' lives. Chapter 3 focused on critical inquiry grounded in personal and community worldview. The emphasis here will be on using the tools of logical reconstruction to address the arguments posed in the advertisement—via the presented skills of argument reconstruction deductively and inductively. Remember from Chapter 3 that, because outlining depends upon various tenets of one's personal worldview and the common body of knowledge from some given community, there may be variations in logical reconstruction. Some of the texture of this is given in the comments after the reconstruction (meant to support a possible pro or con evaluation).

The Media[1]

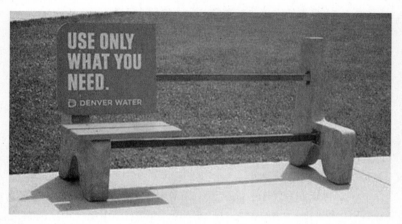

Comment: The point of contention in this visual argument (that we ought to reduce water consumption by two-thirds) is supported by the principle of analogy that works to support an inductive generalization that conservation of water (and perhaps other natural resources) is a goal we should strive to achieve. The mechanics of the analogy are:

1. The bench presented is two-thirds gone, yet there is enough to sit on—(fact)

2. The essential function of a bench is to provide a place to sit—(fact)

[3. Satisfying a good's essential function is all we ought to concern ourselves with—(fact)]

4. We only need a third of the bench to sit on—(1–3)

5. The dynamics of the bench are just like the function-utilization of natural resources such as water—(assertion)

6. We can reduce water consumption by two-thirds and still satisfy essential function—(4, 5)

---

7. We ought to reduce water consumption by two-thirds—(4, 6)

This argument has at least two controversial premises. Premise 3 is a principle of minimal functionalism set in moral, ecological terms. Objectors might say that minimal satisfaction should not be the standard, but optimal resource usage for the benefit of humans. According to this viewpoint, we should exploit our resources to the fullest to help humans right now with longer showers, regular toilets, watering of residential lawns, and the use of potable water for irrigation (contra the rest of the world).

Premise 5 states the inductive analogy that allows the generalization. If bench-sitting is unlike water usage, then the conclusion drawn will not be valid or cogent.

Comment: This ad uses analogy to support its point of contention that we should change our attitude toward those with HIV/AIDS from one of exclusion to one of compassion and care. The context is how the common body of knowledge views those infected with HIV/AIDS. The viewpoint is that these individuals are marginalized just like a person walking in a bubble physically cut off from the community.

1. People with HIV/AIDS are shunned from the community—(fact)
[2. People with HIV/AIDS have a treatable though fatal disease—(fact)]
[3. All those with treatable though fatal diseases deserve inclusive compassion and care—(assertion)]
4. People with HIV/AIDS should be given compassion and care—(1–3)

5. In fact, people with HIV/AIDS are treated as if they lived in the bubble of the "other," excluded from compassion and care—(assertion)

6. We should change our attitude toward those with HIV/AIDS from one of exclusion to one of compassion and care—(4, 5)

Comment: This ad confronts a public health problem with a vehicle of public transportation. The analogy that seeks to generate the generalization is that, just as the bus emits noxious emissions that we all agree smell and are bad, so also smokers take on an internal sort of pollution that is killing them. The point of contention is that it is time to stop smoking before you pollute yourself to death.

1. The bus is polluting the atmosphere with its noxious smoke—(fact)
2. The cigarette picture mimics the smoker's own exhaling to the bus's exhaust—(fact)
[3. Just as the bus pollutes the environment, so also does a cigarette smoker pollute his own internal environment: his body—(assertion)]
[4. Pollution of any sort is wrong—(assertion)]
[5. Wrong actions should be changed—(assertion)]

---

6. Cigarette smokers should quit—(1–5)

Phishing

Dear Maria,
Congratulations! You are the winner of a random Internet lottery that is sponsored by Fortune 500 companies to draw new interest in their products. For more information about your prize, click on the following link: http://www.internetwinners@Fortune500promotion.com.

Next screen:

Congratulations! In order to claim your prize of $100,000, you need to provide the following information:
    Name:
    Address:
    Name of Bank:

Account Number:

Any Password:

Social Security Number:

(We are required under law to report your earnings to the Internal Revenue Service.)

Comment: The illogic of this presentation can be set out as follows.

1. All legitimate contests are entered into by some voluntary act—(fact)
2. I did not voluntarily enter this contest—(fact)
3. This contest is not legitimate—(1, 2)
4. The information requested is private financial information—(fact)
5. Private financial information in the wrong hands can cause fraud—(fact)
6. Fraud against me can cost me money—(fact)
[7. I don't want to lose money to a con man—(fact)]

---

8. I should not respond to this request—(3–7)

Once one sets out logically what is the probable outcome of this solicitation, it becomes very clear that this is not a transaction in which to engage. Press the delete key on your Web browser.

Exercises

Create logical outlines for the inductive and deductive arguments you see demonstrated in the following four media presentations.

Exercise 1

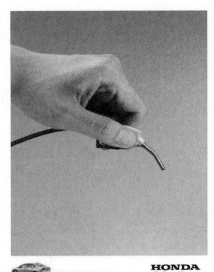

Exercise 2

Exercise 3

Exercise 4

Phishing Message

Dear Friend,

I am the lawyer for Suzy Nasouli, who was recently forced to leave the country, but cannot get her money out. We need a third party who has an American bank account in order to transfer the funds, $34 million. This was money that came from the Nasouli family mining fortune. It would be terrible for this money to be lost and Ms. Nasouli to become destitute. I implore you to help us avoid this disaster. In order to thank you for your help, I have been authorized to offer you $5 million as a fee. Please contact me at your earliest convenience: ABC@yahoo.com.

Yours truly,

Bagavier Tasman, Esq.

Attorney at Law

Notes

1. Source: http://justcreativedesign.com/2008/07/30/192 -of-the-best-smart-clever-creative-advertisements. Accessed November 1, 2008.

PART THREE

RESPONDING TO THE TEXT

CHAPTER 7

Finding Out
What You Believe

An *evaluation* is a reasoned response to a logical argument. This reasoned response takes a point of view that can be seen as supporting the argument or not. The former response will be called a *pro* evaluation and the latter a *con* evaluation. Chapters 8 and 9 will concentrate on the mechanics of how to construct each. This chapter will give an overview of some of the elements that make up this form of argumentation through the creation of a pre-essay packet that will make you more successful at it.

The first thing an evaluation needs is structure. Without structure, by which its remarks may be guided, an evaluation becomes meaningless. As was said earlier about movies (see Introduction), general statements that do not make their measurement scale explicit yield no useful information.

Sometimes they are worse than nothing because they *can* make things unclear.

An evaluation must (a) make clear the assessed character of that which is being evaluated (an argument, book, opera, movie, and so on); (b) analyze that character into its components; (c) direct attention to particular important components; (d) put forth a point of view directed through those components; (e) generate a reasoned argument for that point of view; and (f) show how one's view of the whole is affected by the positions taken on those components. This is a tall order. Let us examine in a little more detail some of these points.

The Process of Argument to This Point

In Chapters 1 and 2 a method of critical reading was set forth that would enable the student to integrate his or her personal worldview and the pervading shared community worldview into his or her experience with the text. The result was to ferret out the point of contention (conclusion) along with the general sense of what supported it. This process was repeated analogically with media examples.

In Chapters 4 and 5 a natural language system of deductive and inductive argument was described that presented precise rules for defining the relation between premises and the conclusion in a more formal fashion. At this point the student has read the text multiple times and reconstructed the main arguments presented in deductive or inductive reconstructions—including enthymemes.

What is left at this stage is to use the outline as the launching pad to create a pre-essay packet that will assist you in fashioning an essay that is pro or con. This chapter will describe the way you create such a packet.

Sample Argument

Consider: There are several sorts of friendships that can be made in life. Each form of friendship owes its existence to a particular category. The categories are utility, pleasure, and goodness. Thus, one sort of friend is someone you interact with because each of you gives the other a tangible, material benefit. This relationship will end as soon as the tangible, material benefit ends. The second form is similar to the first. The benefit, however, is immaterial: pleasure. Because of its immaterial nature, some interaction between the essential worldviews of the participants occurs. However, like utility, when the pleasure ends, so does the relationship. The final form is goodness. In this sort of friendship, it is the ability of each reciprocally to improve the moral excellence of the other that occasions the relationship. When you are with such a friend, then you know that you are better, becoming all that you can be. Each individual is permanently affected for the better. Thus, the friendship based upon goodness is the best sort of friendship.

This is a paraphrase of an argument that Aristotle presents in Book Eight of the *Nicomachean Ethics*. Treat this as your assignment.

Okay. Let's apply the process:

1. Read the passage for overall meaning.
2. Find the principal claim—The best sort of friend-ship is one based upon goodness.
3. What is the evidence for the claim?
4. Put the evidence into logical form using the methodology advocated in Chapter 4.

Start by writing down the conclusion. Then find sub-conclusions that may support it.

Conclusion: The best sort of friendship is one based upon goodness. (principal claim)

Subconclusions:

1. There are three sorts of friendship: those based on utility, those based on pleasure, and those based on goodness—(assertion)
2. Utility fails when the utility ends—(fact)
3. Pleasure fails when the pleasure ends—(fact)
4. Pleasure does interactively touch the worldviews of the participants—(assertion)
5. Interactive goodness makes each party more excellent—(assertion)
6. Each individual is permanently affected for the better—(assertion)

Enthymemes necessary for the inferences are:

1. Long-term relationships are better than short-term ones—(assertion)

2. Interactive touching of worldviews is a worthwhile and positive event—(assertion)
3. All of us, by nature, desire most of all to be more excellent—(assertion)
4. Goodness and its expression are long-term—(assertion)

From these observations we are prepared to outline the argument according to form[1]:

1. There are three sorts of friendships: those based on utility, those based on pleasure, and those based on goodness—(assertion)
2. Utility friendships fail when the benefit that is the basis of the friendship ends—(fact)
[3. Long-term relationships are better than short-term ones—(assertion)]
[4. Changes in utility are frequent and characteristic of a short-term relationship—(assertion)]
5. Utility friendships are not the best—(1–4)
6. Pleasure relationships fail when the pleasure ends—(fact)
7. Pleasure relationships interactively touch the worldviews of the participants—(assertion)
[8. Interactive touching of worldviews is a worthwhile and positive event—(assertion)]
9. Pleasure relationships are not the best, but they are better than utility friendships—(3, 6, 7, 8)

10. Goodness relationships are characterized by inter-active goodness—(assertion)
11. Interactive goodness makes all parties perma-nently more excellent—(assertion)
[12. All of us, by nature, desire most of all to be more excellent—(fact)]
[13. Goodness and its expression are long-term—(assertion)]
14. Goodness relationships are better than those based upon pleasure—(9–13)

---

15. The best sort of friendship is one based upon goodness—(5, 9, 14)

This is an example of a logical outline according to the rules provided. So, the first piece in your pre-essay packet is your outline of the author's argument.

Deciding Which Premises to Focus On

Once there is an outline, one must examine the various premises, beginning with those justified by assertion. Assertion is the weakest form of justification; therefore, one is most likely to find in an assertion the particular, important component toward which the reader wishes to direct attention.

What is especially important at this point is to view such premises in a *pluralistic context*. This is a context in which many viewpoints regarding that single element might be brought forth. It is very important that one not allow a strong personal feeling to mask all the possible reasons one might be inclined to accept or reject this particular premise. The reason for this pluralism is that it allows a more comprehensive vision of the assertion.

You cannot know why you are for or against a single tenet until you understand fully all the various reasons others give for their assent or dissent. Thus, this pluralistic appraisal of the premise is extremely important in developing an informed view of its truth or falsity.

Obviously, such a process is time-consuming. One must limit the number of premises under consideration. The two guides that should rule such choices are (a) the crucial nature of the premise, and (b) the controversial nature of the premise. These guides act serially; in other words, we apply (a) before (b). One needs first to examine the premise(s) that is crucial to the argument. Is it correct or not? If the reviewer is in any doubt, he or she should apply the pluralism principle in order to help decide.

Among several *crucial* premises that may be isolated, the *controversial* nature of a premise should narrow one's choice. This is true because one will need to develop a position on such a premise more fully, since it is the one to which most reviewers will naturally gravitate.

An example can be seen in the sample argument. According to the two criteria above, we must first examine the crucial premises and then the controversial ones. The concept of being *crucial* is relative to the inferences that are drawn. In order that we not simply list all premises justified as *assertion* or *fact*, a good process of inquiry is to list those premises that are used to generate inferences and group them according to similar messages. In this argument the following premises stand out as groups on the same topic:

First Group—Initial Classification
  1. There are three sorts of friendships occasioned by utility, pleasure, and goodness—(assertion)

Second Group—Link between Better and "Long-Term"
  2. Utility friendships fail when the benefit that is the basis of the friendship ends—(fact)
  [3. Long-term relationships are better than short-term ones—(assertion)]
  [4. Changes in utility are frequent and characteristic of a short-term relationship—(assertion)]
  6. Pleasure relationships fail when the pleasure ends—(fact)
  [7. Goodness and its expression are long-term—(assertion)]

Third Group—Interactivity of Friends as a Positive Excellence
  8. Pleasure relationships interactively touch the world-views of the participants—(assertion)
  [9. Interactive touching of worldviews is a worthwhile and positive event—(assertion)]
  10. Goodness relationships are characterized by interactive goodness—(assertion)
  11. Interactive goodness makes all parties permanently more excellent—(assertion)
  [12. All of us, by nature, desire most of all to be more excellent—(fact)]

Obviously, this process is very subjective. One reader might create one sort of grouping while another might group via different criteria. However, subjectivity in this case is good because you are the one writing the essay. Thus, one looks at the groups he has created using the criterion of being crucial and then decides which premises are most controversial (meaning those that he thinks are logically prior [crucial] and those that he might have the most to say [controversial]). For example, in the above grouping one student might decide that the first group is not very promising. Then, in the second group he might choose premise 3, and in the third group he might choose premise 11. *The number of premises you choose to write on is dictated by the length of your proposed essay.* For example, in my classes I often assign a short, 750-word essay (around two and a half pages). For such a short essay two premises are probably the maximum that one can adequately develop. The longest argumentative paper I assign at the undergraduate level is a 2,400-word essay (around eight pages). In the case of the eight-page essay, choosing three premises is generally more serviceable.

Creating Brainstorming Sheets

Once one has isolated his two or three premises, then the process of brainstorming begins. At the top of a sheet of paper (or your computer screen), list all the things that strike you about the premise both in favor and against (pro and con). Then do the same for your other premises. Each premise gets its own separate sheet of paper. For example, from our sample one might begin with premise 3.[2]

[3. Long-term relationships are better than short-term ones—(assertion)]

Pro Thoughts:

- In life we generally value a good if it lasts longer: cars, appliances, clothes, and so on. Perhaps the same is true of friendship.
- Longevity of anything is connected to how well it is constructed. We all value that which is well constructed over that which is less well constructed. Thus, a well-constructed friendship is the best kind.
- Some who endorse spiritual values in life connect a spiritual element to God and immortality. Immortality is a concept about the infinitely long-term. Perhaps by analogy, a long-term friendship based upon goodness may be connected to this community worldview?

Con Thoughts:

- Life is transitory. One should seize the day and find pleasure in the moment rather than losing something nice in the vain search for the long-term.
- High intensity of feeling is to be preferred over low intensity. This is a more relevant standard of value. High intensity is hard (if not impossible) to maintain in the long run—thus temporary short-term pleasure that is intense is to be preferred over long-term, more permanent, low-intensity relationships.
- Most Taoists and Buddhists do not hold out for the immortal. They believe it is a spiritual illusion. Thus, looking for the permanent is a fool's game that leads one away from (rather than toward) spiritual truth.

The brainstorming sheets can (and should) be more extensive than the above sample. The sample is provided as an example of how the brainstorming sheet should look. In our sample pre-essay packet, the student should repeat the brainstorming sheet on another page for premise 11. (Hint: Most people cannot create effective brainstorming sheets at one sitting. Try scheduling at least three different times when you can work on them. If you are a social learner, you might consider entering into discussion with a classmate, friend, or family member about the truth of the premise from both sides. Tape-record your efforts and then transcribe them onto a page for each premise.)

Once you have created your brainstorming sheets, the next step is to evaluate whether what you wrote leans more to the *pro* or to the *con* position. There are only two accepted stances for the argumentative essay according to this book: the pro and the con. Now is the time to choose. Sometimes the choice is easy. You have many more bullet points for *pro* than for *con*. Then the choice is easy. However, on the sample brainstorming sheet there are an equal number of points on each side. In those cases, you simply have to appeal to your personal and community worldview perspectives and choose one over the other. For purposes of illustration, let us assume that the *pro* position was chosen.

Finishing the Pre-Essay Packet: Creating the Cover Sheet

The final step for our pre-essay preparation is to create a cover sheet for the packet. This is the last step in the order

Evaluation of Aristotle's Argument on Friendship

Pro Thoughts:

Possible *objections* to the argument: premise [3. Long-term relationships are better than short term ones—(assertion)]

- Life is transitory. One should seize the day and find pleasure in the moment.
- High intensity of feeling is to be preferred over low intensity.
- Most Taoists and Buddhists do not hold out for the immortal; they consider immortality a spiritual illusion.

Replies to the objections to premise 3:

- In life we generally value as good that which lasts longer.
- Longevity of anything is connected to how well it is constructed.
- Some who endorse spiritual values in life connect a spiritual element to God and immortality. Immortality is a concept about the infinitely long-term. Perhaps by analogy, a long-term friendship based upon goodness may be connected to this community worldview.

Objections and replies to premise 11: Interactive goodness makes all parties permanently more excellent—(assertion)

Introduction: Aristotle argues in Book Eight of the *Nicomachean Ethics* that the best sort of friendship is one based upon goodness. He bases this argument upon two controversial premises: (a) Long-term relationships are better than short-term ones, and (b) interactive goodness makes all parties permanently more excellent. It is here that detractors will focus their attention. This essay will examine the strength of these objections in order and then show them to be mistaken, thus supporting Aristotle's general conclusion.

of creation, but it is the first step in the order of logical presentation. The elements that should be on the cover sheet include: (a) some identification of the argument, (b) the argumentative stance of the essay (pro or con), (c) the principal points to be addressed in the body of the essay, and (d) the actual introduction you intend to use in your essay.

The cover sheet and the packet that is behind it (the outline and the brainstorming sheets) constitute your roadmap to guide your critical response to the argumentative text. One maxim I often repeat to my students is that effective essays are the endpoint of a process of critical inquiry. When this process occurs thoughtfully over time, the end result (the essay) is of a markedly higher quality. Here is an example of a cover sheet for the sample argument.

The Elements of a
Finished Pre-Essay Packet

A finished pre-essay packet should contain the following elements:[3]

- Cover Page
- Brainstorming Sheets
- Outline of the Argument

I suggest that the pre-essay packet be turned in along with the essay. Only the essay is graded, but the pre-essay packet provides the professor with a strong diagnostic tool for helping students improve on their next essay.

Reading Questions

1. What are some of the general purposes of any evaluation?
2. How do we accomplish making the assessed character of the argument clear and then analyzing this into its components?
3. How does one decide on which premise to focus?
4. What is a crucial premise for evaluation?
5. What is a controversial premise?
6. What is a brainstorming sheet and how does one create one?
7. What elements should be listed on the cover sheet?
8. What elements should be in the pre-essay packet?

Notes

1. I should note that I generally require students to put down the numbers of pages where they found various premises.

2. I have used bullet points for the sample brainstorming sheet. However, many of my students have used other methods—such as creating trees or fences with the thoughts as written on the page by hand. This method integrates design with the expression of thoughts. If you are graphically talented, this might be a good strategy for you. Whatever unlocks your critical imagination is what you should employ. Trial and error should show you what is best for you.

3. Some instructors may want to create their own versions of the important arguments they want students to reconstruct.

In this case I suggest uploading these onto course intranet tools such as Blackboard *after* students have made their first attempt at the argument. In these cases, I require students to create an integrated outline combining aspects of the professor's outline along with their original efforts. All three outlines should be included in the pre-essay packet.

CHAPTER 8

The Con Essay

This chapter will set out the general strategy of writing a con essay. We will follow from the sample argument from Aristotle set out in Chapter 7. In the next chapter the general strategy of the pro essay is set out.

The flow of the con essay is as follows:

Introduction
Statement of Objections
Anticipation of and Refutation of Rebuttals
Theoretical Observations
Significance of the Argument

Introduction

The introduction should have the following elements: identification of the conclusion being examined, the key premises (chosen on the basis of their being crucial and controversial), the statement of authorial standpoint (in this case, *con*), and a short statement on essay strategy.

In the sample argument set out in Chapter 7, an introduction that fulfills these requirements would read like this:

Sample Introduction—Paragraph 1

Aristotle argues in Book Eight of the *Nicomachean Ethics* that the best sort of friendship is one based upon goodness. He bases this argument upon two objectionable premises: (a) Long-term relationships are better than short-term ones, and (b) interactive goodness makes all parties permanently more excellent. This essay will examine these pivotal premises and show them to be false, thus rendering Aristotle's general conclusion as unproven.

This paragraph is only a model, but a few comments are in order. In the argumentative essay (especially the 750-word through 2,400-word model), it is important to be efficient with one's introduction. There is no need to give too much background information that is irrelevant to exploring the argument at hand.

Statement of Objections

The statement of objections should have the following elements: (a) a critical reading of the premise at hand, (b) a short list of surface objections, and (c) how the surface objections really reveal deep problems. (This procedure should be re-

peated for each premise examined—remember to change
paragraphs when you change your focus to another premise.)

Sample Objection to One Premise—
Paragraphs 2 and 3

[Critical Reading of Premise] Aristotle asserts the objectionable premise that long-term relationships are better
than short-term ones. This essay will interpret this to
mean that one should avoid possible highly pleasurable
transitory relationships in favor of the search for deeper,
more lasting relationships. [A Short List of Surface Ob-
jections] It is the position of this essay that such a premise
is flawed. This is because: (a) Life is transitory. One should
seize the day and find pleasure in the moment rather than
losing something nice in the vain search for the long-term;
(b) High intensity of feeling is to be preferred over low intensity. This is a more relevant standard of value. High
intensity is hard (if not impossible) to maintain in the long
run—thus temporary, short-term pleasure that is intense is
to be preferred over long-term, more permanent, low-
intensity relationships; and (c) Most Taoists and Buddhists
do not hold out for the immortal. They believe it is a spiritual illusion. Thus, looking for the permanent is a fool's
game that leads one away from (rather than toward) spiritual truth.

[How Surface Objections Reveal Deep Problems]
Let us begin by examining our attitude toward the transitory nature of life. On the one hand, some might seek some

outlets of immortality—such as art. Hippocrates said, "Life is short, Art is long." How are we to deal with the transitory nature of life? One way is to escape into the delusion of long-term friendship possibilities. This is a ruse. Life is short. We must grab for the pleasure and satisfaction wherever we may find it. Tomorrow we may be dead. To seek for a tomorrow that may never happen is to marry an illusion. You live right now. You have a potential for happiness right now. Why is there a question of what to do? [The student should continue on and cover (b) and (c) above through how those surface objections reveal deep problems.]

Anticipation of and Refutation of Rebuttals

The anticipations of and refutation of rebuttals should have these components: (a) the best possible argument that can be made against your surface objections, and (b) the best possible argument that can be made against the deeper problems.

Sample of Anticipation and Refutation of Rebuttals—Mid-Essay

Now Aristotle might disagree with my response on this key premise. He might say that though life is transitory, this is not a reason to abandon a strategy toward long-term values over those at the moment. He might say that given our short time on Earth, we should be even more aware of making the most of what we are capable of. A person of excellence is striving toward a long-term goal via moderation regardless of his or her amount of time on Earth.

But Aristotle is surely wrong here. It is just as possible that the opposite is true. Aristotle stacks the deck in favor of his theory of moderation and excellence. These are not argued for, but are assumed to be, self-evidently true. But nothing could be further from the case. This author's critical statements are a case in point. It is just as intuitively plausible that living in the moment and for the moment is what is excellent. In this case *excellent* refers to being unburdened and free to explore the possibilities that each day presents. Since intuition is the ultimate ground for each claim, Aristotle cannot claim firmer grounding for his account. [Repeat the anticipation and refutation of rebuttals for the other premises.]

Theoretical Observations

Now transform your rebuttals to their more theoretical expressions.

Sample of Theoretical Observations— Toward the End of the Essay

Metaphysically, we must see ourselves as fragile beings in a dance before death. It is all about to end soon or not. Regardless, we must act on that possibility. Why delay and postpone for what probably never will be? Hard-core, empirical engagement of the *now* dictates that we make of it what we can. Life must be lived in the moment.

Significance of Argument

Now discuss the argument's significance and its relevance today.

Sample Significance of the Argument—Last Paragraph

Today's society offers an important context for accepting or rejecting Aristotle's account of friendship. Aristotle wants to elevate friendship to an interactive striving for the good. To this end he employs the controversial premises: (a) long-term relationships are better than short-term ones, and (b) interactive goodness makes all parties permanently more excellent. This essay has shown these both to be false. Instead, it has been suggested that pleasure and spontaneity (as opposed to slogging after goodness) is to be preferred as a model of friendship and of living one's life. So much of modern life is planned out for you: What courses you take in high school and your activities are all directed toward college. Once you reach college it is all about getting a job or going to graduate school. When is a person supposed to have fun? If we always live for the long-term future ahead of us, then we put off who we really are until then—if we live that long. A better alternative is to engage in the present. Do not look to tomorrow for the answer. Friendship is like holding a bird in one's hand. For one to appreciate the bird one must lay open his grasp so that he might enjoy the bird. However, by opening the hand, the bird may flee at any moment. That's what is always at risk. But the possibility of the union disintegrating gives it a potent intensity. Forget tomorrow. There is freedom in the present and in the pleasure that one may find. These are the only friendships worth having.

Common Mistakes

In my teaching this method over the years, I have encountered these common mistakes:

- Writing long and flowery introductions.
- The objections are not fully developed. They often stop at the surface arguments and do not proceed to the deeper problems.
- Students often run the premises and objections together, mixing them. This creates confusion on the part of the reader. It is important to label what you are doing so that the reader understands clearly your orderly progression.
- Anticipation and refutation of rebuttals. Many students bring up weak counterstatements. They want so much to defeat the author that they are reticent to really consider the question from that viewpoint. This is not intellectually honest. Try to stretch yourself by empathetically projecting yourself into the other standpoint.

- Theoretical observations. Try to arrive at the logically antecedent causes that explain the underlying reason that you believe the way you do. This is hard work. There is a tendency to view the problem at the same level as the argument you are considering, rather than at the level of some tenet that is more foundational.

CHAPTER 9

The Pro Essay

This chapter will set out the general strategy of writing a pro essay. We will follow from the sample argument from Aristotle set out in Chapter 7.

The flow of the pro essay is as follows:

Introduction
Objectors to Key Premises
Replies to the Objections
Theoretical Observations
Significance of the Argument

Let's examine each of these in order.

Introduction

The introduction should have the following elements: identification of the conclusion being examined, the key premises (chosen on the basis of their being crucial and controversial), the statement of authorial standpoint (in this case *pro*), and a short statement on essay strategy.

In the sample argument set out in Chapter 7, an introduction that fulfills these requirements would read like this:

Sample Introduction—Paragraph 1

Aristotle argues in Book VIII of the *Nicomachean Ethics* that the best sort of friendship is one based upon goodness. He bases this argument upon two controversial premises: (a) Long-term relationships are better than short-term ones, and (b) interactive goodness makes all parties permanently more excellent. It is here that detractors will focus their attention. This essay will examine the strength of these objections in order and then show them to be mistaken, thus supporting Aristotle's general conclusion.

This paragraph is only a model, but a few comments are in order. In the argumentative essay (especially the 750-word through 2,400-word model), it is important to be efficient with one's introduction. There is no need to give too much background information that is irrelevant to exploring the argument at hand.

Objectors to Key Premises

The statement of objections should have the following elements: (a) a critical reading of the premise at hand, (b) a short list of surface objections, and (c) how the surface objections really reveal deep problems. [This procedure should be repeated for each premise examined. Remember to change paragraphs when you change your focus to another premise.]

Sample Objection to One
Premise—Paragraphs 2 and 3

[**Critical Reading of Premise**] Aristotle's detractors might object to the controversial premise that long-term relationships are better than short-term ones. This essay will interpret this to mean that one should avoid possible highly pleasurable, transitory relationships in favor of the search for deeper, more lasting relationships. [**A Short List of Surface Objections**] Objectors here might contend that such a premise is flawed. This is because: (a) Life is transitory. One should seize the day and find pleasure in the moment, rather than losing something nice in the vain search for the long-term; (b) High intensity of feeling is to be preferred over low intensity. This is a more relevant standard of value. High intensity is hard (if not impossible) to maintain in the long run—thus temporary, short-term pleasure that is intense is to be preferred over long-term, more permanent, low-intensity relationships; and (c) Most Taoists and Buddhists do not hold out for the immortal. They believe it is a spiritual illusion. Thus, looking for the permanent is a fool's game that leads one away from (rather than toward) spiritual truth.

[How Surface Objections Reveal Deep Problems]
Let us begin by examining the objector's attitude toward the transitory nature of life. On the one hand, some might seek some outlets of immortality—such as art. Hippocrates said, "Life is short, Art is long." How are we to deal with the transitory nature of life? One way is to escape into the delusion of long-term possibilities of friendship. This is a ruse. Life is short. We must grab for the pleasure and satisfaction wherever we may find it. Tomorrow we may be dead. To seek for a tomorrow that may never happen is to marry an illusion. You live right now. You have a potential for happiness right now. Why is there a question of what to do? [The student should continue on and cover (b) and (c) above through how those surface objections—on the part of the sample objector—reveal deep problems.]

Replies to the Objections

The replies to the objections should have these components: (a) the best possible argument that can be made against your surface objections, and (b) the best possible argument that can be made against the deeper problems.

Sample Reply to One Premise—Mid-Essay

The objections raised are significant. If they are correct, Aristotle's argument will certainly fail. However, this essay seeks to defend Aristotle. Let's address these various objections in order. First, though the objector argues that life is transitory, this is not a reason to abandon a strategy toward long-term values over those at the moment. Given our short time on Earth, we should be even more aware of making the most of what we are capable of. A shortness of time does not mean that we should disregard time and become libertines, but rather that we should take the intensity of our brief lives as a clarion to develop ourselves according to our highest capacities. A person of excellence is striving toward a long-term goal via moderation regardless of his or her amount of time on Earth. This is what Aristotle meant when he opened the *Ethics* with an exhortation to look for the good as the end to which all things naturally strive. Even if we are not long for this world, the principles of what makes a human life valuable (including its friendships) transcend any of our individual existences. We value them *because* they show us a preferable path to happiness. [The student should repeat replies to the other objections.]

Theoretical Observations

Now transform your replies into theoretical observations.

Sample of Theoretical Observations— Toward the End of the Essay

In today's society so much is full of frenetic change. What is true on Monday may be false on Friday. Can people effectively live this way? Aristotle suggests a different route: friendship based upon making each other better. To this end he creates an argument with the controversial premises:

(a) Long-term relationships are better than short-term ones, and (b) interactive goodness makes all parties permanently more excellent. There are really two key issues here: permanence and the value of embracing the good with another person. In the first instance, if we are to have values that are worth living for, they cannot be so flimsy that they disappear as soon as they come, like the first frost of winter. Most people recognize the value of permanence so that we strive for it in all we do—such as saving for a house, looking for a career rather than a mere job, and choosing a style of life that balances the soul for the long term. In the second instance, Aristotle recognizes that we are social animals who need to share. In friendship, what could be higher than sharing goodness? By doing this we both improve and share in the experience of actualizing each other toward ultimate human goals: human excellence that confers deep happiness. These are the foundational truths that lie behind Aristotle's presentation.

Significance of the Argument

Now discuss the argument's significance and its relevance today.

Sample Significance of the
Argument—Last Paragraph

We stand at a crossroads in today's world. Either we head down the way to superficial pleasures and temporary sensory stimulation or we set out toward a road that is harder in the short term but gets us to a more worthy destination. The substantial is always the best choice. This is true in the friendships we cultivate. Friendships built upon the good will last a lifetime. When we are confronted with personal challenges in which we cease to be able to deliver utility or pleasure to another, it is only the friendship based upon goodness that will see us through difficult times. And because of reciprocity, we also welcome the chance to serve our true friends as well. These are substantial principles upon which a strong and enduring society can be built. It is as true today as when Aristotle wrote his book almost 2,500 years ago.

Common Mistakes

- Writing long and flowery introductions.
- Setting out weak objectors that are not developed beyond quick surface objections.
- Running your objections and your replies together. Make it clear (by using new paragraphs and by labeling) where you are in the essay.
- Not really answering the objector. Often the objections and replies sit on two mutually exclusive planets and never interact. To solve this, imagine you are a lawyer in the courtroom of truth and arguing for your client, Aristotle, against possible attacks.
- Underdevelopment. Look to your brainstorming sheets to ensure you have fully said what you believe is important to say.

APPENDIX

The Big Picture

The purpose of this appendix is to fill in a few gaps by providing additional contexts in which outlines can be used to unlock the structures of various argumentative texts. As always, the general execution of this task will be suggestive rather than comprehensive.

Micro- and Macro-Arguments

Throughout this primer the emphasis has been on outlining arguments that occur in several paragraphs or at most in a few pages. Such arguments are the atomic building blocks upon which larger arguments may be constructed. In this way the conclusions from small arguments become premises for larger arguments. For example, a chapter itself might have an argumentative structure. Such an argument could be outlined using the same techniques described in

Chapter 4. The main difference is that the text is of greater length and the references to the premises are less explicit. For this reason the best way to prepare for outlining the macro-argument is to begin with outlines of the micro-arguments contained within it.

The larger argument emerges from the conclusions of the various micro-arguments. In this way understanding the macro-argument involves apprehending the relationship of the atomic micro-arguments. It is this larger structure that affords a deeper understanding of what an author is trying to say. One's reconstruction of the macro-argument may involve some tampering with the micro-arguments according to the principle of fairness set out in Chapter 4. The parts influence our understanding of the whole and vice versa. This dynamic tension between part and whole allows a fuller understanding of context in accordance with the pluralism principle.

FIGURE A.1: Macro- and Micro-Arguments

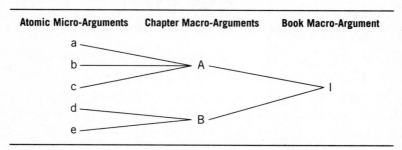

Sometimes a whole book has an argument that may be reconstructed from the chapter arguments. The difference lies in the levels of generality involved. As one describes a progressively larger and larger section of text, the premises of the macro-arguments themselves come from increasingly general sections of text. These relations are pictorially depicted in Figure A.1.

The same types of dynamic interaction can occur between chapter macro-arguments and book macro-arguments. This complicates the contextual fabric and thus enhances comprehension through the pluralism principle.

Examples of this level of argument are difficult to present in a slim volume such as this because of space constraints. However, some flavor for the macro-argument can be presented through an examination of the Declaration of Independence. This level of macro-argument more closely resembles the chapter-level macro-argument.

Example One
The Unanimous Declaration of the
Thirteen United States of America

When in the Course of human events, it becomes necessary for one People to dissolve the political bands which have connected them with another, and to assume among the powers of the earth, the separate and equal station to which the Laws of Nature and of Nature's God entitle them, a decent respect to the opinions of mankind requires that they should declare the causes which impel them to the separation.

We hold these truths to be self-evident, that all men are created equal, that they are endowed by their Creator with certain unalienable Rights, that among these are Life,

Liberty, and the pursuit of Happiness—That to secure these rights, Governments are instituted among Men, deriving their just powers from the consent of the governed, that whenever any Form of Government becomes destructive of these ends, it is the Right of the People to alter or to abolish it, and to institute new Government, laying its foundation on such principles, and organizing its powers in such form, as to them shall seem most likely to effect their Safety and Happiness. Prudence, indeed, will dictate that Governments long established should not be changed for light and transient causes; and accordingly all experience hath shewn, that mankind are more disposed to suffer, while evils are sufferable, than to right themselves by abolishing the forms to which they are accustomed. But when a long train of abuses and usurpations, pursuing invariably the same object, evinces a design to reduce them under absolute despotism, it is their right, it is their duty, to throw off such government, and to provide new Guards for their future security. Such has been the patient Sufferance of these Colonies; and such is now the necessity which constrains them to alter their former Systems of Government. The history of the present King of Great Britain is a history of repeated injuries and usurpations, all having in direct object the establishment of an absolute Tyranny over these States. To prove this, let Facts be submitted to a candid world.

He has refused his Assent to Laws, the most wholesome and necessary for the public good.

He has forbidden his Governors to pass Laws of immediate and pressing Importance, unless suspended in their operation till his assent should be obtained; and when so suspended, he has utterly neglected to attend to them.

He has refused to pass other Laws for the Accommodation of large Districts of People, unless those People would relinquish the Right of Representation in the Legislature, a Right inestimable to them, and formidable to Tyrants only.

He has called together legislative bodies at places unusual, uncomfortable, and distant from the Depository of their Public Records, for the sole purpose of fatiguing them into compliance with his measures.

He has dissolved Representative Houses repeatedly, for opposing with manly firmness his Invasions on the rights of the people.

He has refused for a long time, after such dissolutions, to cause others to be elected; whereby the Legislative Powers, incapable of Annihilation, have returned to the People at large for their exercise; the State remaining in the mean time exposed to all the dangers of invasion from without, and convulsions within.

He has endeavoured to prevent the population of these States; for that purpose obstructing the Laws for Naturalization of Foreigners; refusing to pass others to encourage their migrations hither, and raising the conditions of new Appropriations of Lands.

He has obstructed the Administration of Justice, by refusing his Assent to Laws for establishing Judiciary Powers.

He has made Judges dependent on his Will alone, for the tenure of their offices, and the amount and payment of their salaries.

He has erected a multitude of new Offices, and sent hither swarms of Officers to harass our People, and eat out their Substance.

He has kept among us, in times of peace, Standing Armies, without the consent of our legislatures.

He has affected to render the Military independent of, and superior to the Civil Power.

He has combined with others to subject us to a Jurisdiction foreign to our Constitution, and unacknowledged by our laws; giving his Assent to their Acts of pretended Legislation:

For quartering large bodies of armed troops among us:

For protecting them, by a mock Trial, from punishment for any Murders which they should commit on the Inhabitants of these States:

For cutting off our Trade with all parts of the world:

For imposing Taxes on us without our Consent:

For depriving us, in many cases, of the benefits of Trial by Jury:

For transporting us beyond Seas to be tried for pretended offences:

For abolishing the free System of English Laws in a neighbouring Province, establishing therein an Arbitrary government, and enlarging its Boundaries, so as to render it at once an example and fit instrument for introducing the same absolute rule into these Colonies:

For taking away our Charters, abolishing our most valuable Laws, and altering fundamentally the Forms of our Governments:

For suspending our own Legislatures, and declaring themselves invested with power to legislate for us in all cases whatsoever.

He has abdicated Government here, by declaring us out of his Protection and waging War against us.

He has plundered our seas, ravaged our coasts, burnt our towns, and destroyed the lives of our people.

He is, at this time, transporting large Armies of foreign Mercenaries to compleat the works of death, desolation, and tyranny, already begun with circumstances of Cruelty and Perfidy, scarcely paralleled in the most barbarous ages, and totally unworthy the Head of a civilized nation.

He has constrained our fellow Citizens taken Captive on the high Seas to bear Arms against their Country, to become the Executioners of their Friends and Brethren, or to fall themselves by their Hands.

He has excited domestic Insurrections amongst us, and has endeavoured to bring on the Inhabitants of our Frontiers, the merciless Indian Savages, whose known rule of warfare, is an undistinguished destruction, of all ages, sexes and conditions.

In every stage of these Oppressions We have Petitioned for Redress in the most humble terms: Our repeated Petitions have been answered only by repeated injury. A Prince, whose character is thus marked by every act which may define a Tyrant, is unfit to be the ruler of a free people.

Nor have We been wanting in attentions to our British brethren. We have warned them from time to time of attempts by their legislature to extend an unwarrantable jurisdiction over us. We have reminded them of the circumstances of our emigration and settlement here. We have appealed to their native justice and magnanimity, and we have conjured them by the ties of our common kindred to disavow these usurpations, which, would inevitably interrupt our connections and correspondence. They too have been deaf to the voice of justice and of consanguinity. We must, therefore, acquiesce in the Necessity, which denounces our Separation, and hold them, as we hold the rest of mankind, Enemies in War, in Peace Friends.

We, therefore, the Representatives of the United States of America, in General Congress, Assembled, appealing to the Supreme Judge of the world for the rectitude of our intentions, do, in the Name, and by Authority of the good People of these Colonies, solemnly publish and declare, That these united Colonies are, and of Right ought to be, Free and Independent States; that they are Absolved from all Allegiance to the British Crown, and that all political connection between them and the State of Great Britain, is and ought to be totally dissolved; and that as Free and Independent States, they have full Power to levy War, conclude Peace, contract Alliances, establish Commerce, and to do all other Acts and Things which Independent States may of right do—And for the support of this declaration, with a firm reliance on the protection of Divine Providence, we mutually pledge to each other our Lives, our Fortunes, and our sacred Honor.

A few of the micro-outlines that may be constructed from this document include:

A.1. A decent respect for mankind requires nations to declare any changes in their sovereignty—(assertion)

[2. America wishes a change in its sovereignty—(fact)]

[3. America has a decent respect for mankind—(assertion)]

---

4. America will now declare its intentions for self-rule—(1–3)

B.1. All humans have unalienable rights to life, liberty, and the pursuit of happiness—(assertion)

2. Governments are established to protect these rights—(assertion)

3. Governments are empowered by the citizens to perform their rightful tasks—(assertion)

---

4. Governments that do not protect rights can be changed by the citizens—(1–3)

C.1. There are high costs to be paid in switching governments—(fact)

2. Prudence dictates choosing the lowest cost, all things being equal—(fact)

---

3. A new government should be established only on serious grounds—(1, 2)

D.1. A new government should be established only on serious grounds—(chain argument from argument C)

2. A long series of abuses under despotic rule constitutes serious grounds—(assertion)

3. A long series of abuses under despotic rule would permit a change in governments—(1, 2)

4. The colonies have suffered a long series of abuses under despotic rule—(assertion)

---

5. The colonies may change governments—(3, 4)

E.[1. A tyrant and a despot are generally characterized by
limiting their subjects' self-determination and inflict-
ing harm upon them—(assertion)]

2. The king of England has refused assent to laws, forbidden governors to pass laws, tried to abolish popular representation, and obstructed the administration
of justice—(fact)

3. The king of England has limited the colonists' self-
determination—(2)

4. The king of England has plundered the seas, ravaged
the coasts, burned the towns, and destroyed the lives
of the colonists—(fact)

5. The king of England has inflicted harm upon his
subjects—(4)

---

6. The king of England is a tyrant and a despot—(1, 3, 5)

F.1. Peaceful methods of resolving political conflict refer
to working through channels—(fact)

2. Colonies have petitioned the crown—(fact)

3. Colonies have warned the crown—(fact)

4. Colonies have used moral suasion—(fact)

---

5. Colonies have tried peaceful methods to resolve their
conflict—(1–4)

G.1. Tyrants and despots are unfit to rule—(assertion)

[2. Every state needs a fit ruler—(fact)]

3. The king of England is a tyrant and a despot to the colonies—(chain argument from E)
4. The king of England is unfit to rule the colonies—(1, 3)

---

5. The colonies need a new government—(2, 4)

H.1. The colonists have tried peaceful methods to resolve their conflict—(chain argument from F)
2. The king of England has lent a deaf ear to their peaceful methods—(fact)
3. The citizens of a country have a right to self-determination—(chain argument from B)
4. Overthrowing the king's rule is the only way to ensure self-determination—(assertion)

---

5. The American colonies may overthrow the king of England's rule—(1–4)

To construct a macro-argument from these eight deductive and inductive arguments, first study the relationships between the arguments. Try to see how all the arguments might fit together into a larger argument that encompasses the general sense of the micro-arguments without going into the specific detail that they do. For example:

I.1. Governments that do not protect rights may be changed by the citizens of that country—(assertion from argument B)
2. A new government should only be established as the result of very serious grounds—(assertion from argument C)

3. Not protecting the rights of one's citizens by a king constitutes very serious grounds—(assertion from argument D)
4. The king of England is a despot and a tyrant—(assertion from argument E)
5. Colonies may change governments—(1–4)
6. Every peaceful avenue should be explored in order for a people to be justified in changing governments—(assertion from argument F)
7. Colonies have used every peaceful avenue to address their grievances but the king has lent a deaf ear—(fact from argument F)
8. Colonies may employ nonpeaceful means to change governments—(6, 7)
9. Despots are unfit to rule—(assertion from argument G)
10. Rulers who lend a deaf ear to legitimate complaints are unfit to rule—(assertion from argument H)
11. The king of England is unfit to rule—(4, 7, 9, 10)

---

12. The colonies may change governments—(5, 8, 11)

Argument I takes a little something from each argument: Sometimes it is from the conclusion of the argument, sometimes it is from a crucial or controversial premise that is key to that micro-argument. It is important, however, that in constructing the macro-argument one pay close attention to representing the general sense of the entire passage. This is a tough task. What better way to accomplish this than by using the detailed micro-arguments at hand?

These chapter arguments, in turn, will be used in a similar way to construct book macro-arguments. In this way one can obtain exact understanding at a general level. This sort of comprehension is the most difficult to acquire. Often, people who pretend to this mastery level are really full of vagueness and ambiguity. They find it hard to acquire the same rigor and precision that are more readily obtained at the microlevel. And since much of a discipline's meaningful discourse takes place on the macrolevel, these critics are often in the position of not being able to clearly distinguish the good remarks from the bad, the appropriate wide-level generalizations from the callow and simplistic.

Macro-level outlining can go a long way toward providing just such a standard and thus can be an appropriate tool for helping students control and understand the form of larger, general-level discourse.

Compare and Contrast

One example of the above can be found in the compare-and-contrast evaluation. As a rule, this sort of standard calls for the student to discover two complementary facets of a macro-argument. Thus, this type of evaluation can serve as an example of the use of macro-argumentation.

Rules

1. Find the appropriate body of text for each author called for in the compare-and-contrast evaluation.

2. Find the micro-outlines that cover the texts mentioned in rule 1.
3. Addressing one author at a time, create chapter- or other-level macro-outline(s) from the body of micro-outlines.
4. When macro-outlines are complete for both authors, compare the outlines side by side. Examine the types of conclusions each is trying to draw.
5. Make a list of associated tenets that attach to these conclusions. This list should be similar to the elemental analysis described in Chapter 7.
6. Put each argument before you. Find the appropriate premises to evaluate according to the procedure described in Chapter 7.
7. Decide what you feel to be right or wrong with each premise, using the procedures discussed in Chapter 7—noting, where necessary, any logical fallacies (Chapter 2).
8. Construct your essay from the viewpoint of the "correct" position (which may be a third alternative), using the authors involved as foils (much in the way that the counterarguments are used in the pro evaluation). The contrast and comparison points are thus to be made *only insofar* as such insights bear upon the "correct" position.

The two authors' premises and conclusions thus become springboards by which the correct view of things is revealed. Mere exposition of the authors (which is where many student essays of this type begin and end) is not sufficient to create an entire essay. Such exposition merely sets the stage for the real action to follow. As props and scenery they are there to enhance the drama—not to be the drama itself.

General Questions

The compare-and-contrast essay is one of many types of general questions. It is always most difficult for students to execute because it presupposes a rigorous limiting of the topic before beginning the essay.

Just because a question is broad in scope does not mean that a tight outline cannot be found to represent it. A good outline always suits the scope of the inquiry. The skill acquired through practice with micro-arguments is easily transferred to macro-arguments.

By completing one's skills at this second level of discourse, one has mastered the essential outlining technique. If this primer is being used in conjunction with various course readings, then this final step can be practiced by using the outlines already completed at the micro level. In my own teaching I often collect and examine several micro-arguments throughout the term and spend some time at the end of the course suggesting to the student ways to put his term's work together through creating various macro-level outlines.

Such a notebook of outlines, though time-consuming to prepare, is invaluable to the student. It provides an in-depth appraisal of some particular text ready for instant review.

Learning how to prepare such rigorous reconstruction of a text allows the student to create an artifact of lasting value. Later, in business or some other profession, the same principles can be used to create hard-hitting reports and management presentations. The practical, applied value of this skill cannot be overemphasized.

For the reader who is not using this as part of another course of study, I would suggest taking some book or article that is of interest or of importance to your work and applying the outlining and evaluation techniques on the micro and macro levels.

Final Remarks

We all want to confront the persuaders of this world with confidence. This modest volume proposes positive steps that can allow one to realize such an aspiration. If we are indeed best defined as thinking, rational animals, and if logic is the language of reason, then mastering the techniques of outlining and evaluation of logical argument is one of the most fundamental activities we can pursue. Competence in outlining and evaluation means that each of us may move one step closer to more fully realizing our humanity. And that's a goal well worth striving for.

Reading Questions

1. What is the difference between a macro- and a micro-argument?

2. How can one analyze a macro-argument with precision?
3. What is the general strategy of compare-and-contrast questions?
4. How should one approach other types of general questions?

GLOSSARY

Accent. A fallacy of ambiguity in which multiple meanings are created due to the inclusion of the passage in an unusual context.

Advertiser image. In pictorial argument, the promotion of the institution itself, as opposed to any particular product from the institution.

Amphiboly. A fallacy of ambiguity in which two or more distinct meanings are created from a poorly formed grammatical structure.

Analogy, Induction by. Analogy rests on the assumption that objects that are similar in certain respects will also be similar in other respects.

Appeal to pity. This fallacy persuades via an emotional appeal.

Argument. An argument consists of at least two sentences, one of which purports logically to follow from the other. There are two large classes of argument: deductive and inductive.

Argumentum ad baculum. See Argument from coercion.

Argumentum ad hominem. See Argument against the speaker.

Argument against the speaker. In this fallacy the argument itself is not attacked. Rather, one critiques the person putting forth the argument. This shifts the ground from where it should be.

Argument from authority. This fallacy has two forms: connected and disconnected. In *disconnected* fallacy, an expert from one field reports on something about which he is not an expert. In *connected* fallacy, one accepts an expert's testimony on a subject that goes beyond the evidence and represents an analysis about something that is not agreed upon even by experts in that field. In this case the listener needs more than one expert's opinion. A logical argument is also required.

Argument from coercion. A fallacy that rests on the premise that might makes right.

Argument from ignorance. This fallacy rests on the notion that a proposition is true simply because it has never been proven false, and vice versa.

Assertion. The weakest justification. It means that the premise is true simply because one person has said it. The truth of the premise may be doubted.

Audience. The people at whom the argument is directed.

Begging the question. A fallacy in which one assumes what one is trying to prove.

Causation, inductive argument. This type of inductive argument seeks to show that a set of antecedent conditions brings about a subsequent set of conditions via a scientifically recognized mechanism.

Changing the question. A fallacy in which one shifts the grounds of the argument from the issue under discussion to another issue for which an answer *is* readily available.

Classification. One of the three divisions of the text. This is a mode of analysis in which classes are created on the basis of a division made in the common body of knowledge. This can become a useful element for the argument (in which case it is included as a fact or assertion), or it can be of no direct importance to the argument (in which case it is included in a topical outline but not in a logical outline).

Cogent argument. An inductive argument in which all inferences are highly probable (strong) and all the premises are true.

Common body of knowledge. One of the elements within the context of argument. It consists of a collection of facts and shared assumptions about what counts as a proper way to relate facts.

Compare and contrast. A form of general evaluation in which a macro-argument provides the structure. The compare-and-contrast essay is a vehicle by which one may illustrate the "correct" position on a given point of contention.

Conclusion. This is what an argument aims for. The conclusion follows logically from the premises. Often, we call such sentences *conclusions* within the finished argument and *points of contention* apart from this environment.

Context of argument. The context of argument contains five elements that comprehensively describe the dynamics of logical persuasion: speaker, audience, point of contention, argument, and common body of knowledge. It may be adapted to pictorial argument as well.

Contradictory opposites. See Opposites.

Contrary opposites. See Opposites.

Controversial premise. A controversial premise is one that seems to have a greater number of disputable elements that are comprised within it.

Crucial premise. A crucial premise is usually an assertion or a group of assertions. Among several candidates the premise(s) that seem(s) logically more fundamental will be taken to be crucial. Thus, from among three premises—A, B, C—if B and C are shown to depend logically upon A, then A is more fundamental and therefore more crucial.

Deductive argument. An argument whose conclusion seeks to follow necessarily from the premises.

Dilemma question. This fallacy focuses attention away from the principal issue by offering false choices.

Dividing the text. The text may be divided into three parts: argument, classification, and side comments.

Enumerative induction. In enumerative induction the strategy is to list all the observed properties of something with the objective of making a generalization about that type of thing.

Equivocation. A fallacy of ambiguity that operates by using one term and assigning two or more meanings to that term and then using whichever meaning suits the purpose—moving back and forth between meanings.

Evaluation of an argument. An evaluation is a reasoned response to a logical argument or to a fallacy. A *pro* response supports the author in question. A *con* evaluation seeks to disprove the author's contention.

Fact. This is the middle-strength justification. It means that most listeners would accept the given truth put forth as objectively correct.

Facts, Disputing of. Facts may be disputed by developing one's examination of the following categories: (1) measurements and standards of the circumstances, including: (a) setting up a measurement standard, (b) measuring by that standard, (2) making value judgments within the standard, and (3) putting the standards into practice.

Fairness, Principle of. Always reconstruct an argument in its strongest form even if it requires correcting trivial errors (though these may be noted elsewhere).

Fallacy of ambiguity. This is a classification of fallacy that contains three subclasses: equivocation, amphiboly, and accent. Ambiguity means that multiple meanings are created so that the author may refer to one at one moment and another at another moment, all to his or her advantage.

Fallacy of composition. A false inference that states that properties properly assigned to the *part* may also be assigned to the *whole.*

Fallacy of division. A false inference that states that properties assigned to the *whole* may also be assigned to the *part.*

Fallacy of repetition. The repetition of some argument does not increase its likelihood of being true.

False cause. A false inference that occurs when there is no good evidence by which to infer a causal relationship.

False inference. A classification of fallacy that occurs when the inferences are drawn through improper exercise of the various rules of deduction and/or induction. There are three subclasses: false cause, composition, and division.

Hasty generalization. This fallacy comes about when a broad conclusion is created from an atypical sample.

Incomplete evidence. A fallacy in which one makes a judgment without having the salient portion of data available. This is because the evidence presented is not exhaustive.

Indirect argument. This form of argument varies from direct argument because, instead of having the point of contention proved positively, the logical complement is disproved, or the possible choices are narrowed to one.

Inference. This is formally the strongest justification. The inference is the vehicle that makes one accept some premise as a result of accepting other premises. The truth of the premise is thus dependent upon the truth of those other premises.

Improper analogy. This fallacy occurs by incorrectly shifting the grounds of argument from properties belonging to one statement to those of another. Generally the former is well-known and beyond dispute, while the latter is controversial. There is no scientific mechanism to legislate this shift.

Interlocking premises. A property of an argument that states that all the premises are represented directly or indirectly in the conclusion's inference.

Justification. A justification is the reason we accept a premise. In this book, the myriad of possible reasons have been simplified into three groups: assertion, fact, and inference.

Logical argument and reading comprehension. Logical outlining requires exact, precise exposition of the mechanics of the argument and is more useful than a topical outline. Such precise reconstruction requires a high level of understanding on the part of the reader.

Logical complements. The argument assumes that if we want to prove a point (thesis), first we can assume its opposite (antithesis) and then show how that opposite leads us into an absurd (false) state of affairs.

Logical fallacy. A bad argument that does not persuade through logic.

Logical outline. A logical outline presents only the arguments within a passage. It carefully highlights premises and conclusions.

Loose inference. Whenever the relationship between a premise justified by inference and those listed to support it is such that this justification can be doubted, then the inference is considered loose. It is used only in deductive arguments.

Macro-argument. The argument contained within larger sections of text—a chapter of a book. Though this section of text is of a grander scale, outlining can still be used to illuminate the structure of the argument for more general evaluation.

Micro-argument. The argument found in short sections of text—anywhere from a few sentences to several pages. This scale of argument stands as the building block of larger macro-arguments.

Opposites. Contradictory opposites: Among two propositions that are contradictory opposites, these two propositions have opposite truth-values. For example, if one is true, then the other must be false. Contrary opposites: Among two propositions that are contrary opposites, one may not know for certain the truth-value of one given any truth-value for the other.

Order of genesis. The order of genesis begins with the conclusion and works to establish premises. These operate as cause and effect, respectively.

Order of logical presentation. In the logical order one begins with premises and works to the conclusion. These operate as cause and effect, respectively.

Persuasion. The act of trying to win another to your point of view.

Pictorial argument. Persuasion that features a visual presentation. Like all argument, it can be valid and sound (strong and cogent) or not. It is often used in advertising.

Point of contention. The exact statement about which you are trying to persuade another. Within a finished argument this is called the conclusion.

Premise. The building block of an argument. Collectively, the premises cause one to accept the conclusion.

Proposition. A declarative sentence with truth-value.

Reductio ad absurdum. See Logical complements.

Remainders. This principle of indirect argument assumes a limited number of cases. One can be shown to be the case if the others are shown not to be the case.

Shifting the grounds. A classification of logical fallacy that moves the focus of attention from the argument in question to something else (or uses something else to generate the conclusion).

Shifting the terms. A class of logical fallacy in which inferences are invalid because the terms themselves have been altered in some way.

Side comments. One of the three divisions of the text. Anything that is not an argument or a classification will be labeled a side comment. This information is more pertinent to a topical outline than to a logical outline.

Social identification. This fallacy relies upon social pressure and a "me, too" principle. It suggests that popular acceptance can be equated with logical correctness.

Sound argument. An argument is sound if it is valid and all the premises are true. When an argument is sound, we must accept the conclusion.

Speaker. The person putting forth the argument.

Suppressed premise. These are premises that are needed to make an inference but are not explicitly made by the writer.

Thematic context. Useful in determining what is a premise and what is a conclusion. By noting the point of the passage, the conclusion should become clear. The premises are the material used to support the conclusion.

Tight inference. Whenever the relationship between a premise justified by "inference" and those listed to support it is such that this justification cannot be doubted, then the inference is tight. Used only in deductive arguments.

Topical outline. A summary of all the key points within a passage.

Valid argument. A deductive argument is valid when all the inferences are tight and all the premises are interlocking. In a valid argument, if one were to accept all the premises, he or she would have to accept the conclusion.

Word clues. Certain words that also aid one in determining what is a premise or a conclusion.

Worldview. Personal: the way a given individual views the world (facts and values). It is controlled by the personal worldview imperative as a device of critical inquiry. For example, *All people must develop a single comprehensive and internally coherent worldview that is good and that we strive to act out in our daily lives.* Community: the general understanding of the facts and values in the world according to the common body of knowledge that each community member has a responsibility to update. For example, *Each agent must contribute to a common body of knowledge that supports the creation of a shared community worldview (that is itself complete, coherent, and good) through which social institutions and their resulting policies might flourish within the constraints of the essential core, commonly held values (ethics, aesthetics, and religion).*

INDEX